BROKEN BUT
Beautiful
How My Scars Healed Me

Julie Anna McClure
Edited by Ellyn Luther

Dear Steffano,

I hope you enjoy this story of my journey. I have enjoyed getting to know you & working with you! I wish you the best of luck with your residency! I know you will be great.

Julie McClain
Dec. 29:15

Dedicated to:

My husband Michael.
Thank you for faithfully being there for me, encouraging me,
loving me, and patiently walking through this journey with me.
I love you and love doing life with you.
and
My parents, Tim and Sharon Robson.
Thank you for unselfishly sacrificing so much to
take care of me. I love you both and would not be
where I am today without your love and care.

Acknowledgments

I want to first acknowledge my family. I want to thank my husband Michael who has daily been my supporter and encourager. I want to thank my parents who sacrificed so much and gave of their time to be there for me. I also want to thank my siblings, Jonathan and Charity, who came long distances to be there for me after the accident as well as my brother Tim and his family who left their ministry to come help take care of me. I also want to thank my cousin Diana and her husband Alan for opening up their home for us to stay so we could be close to UAB. Also, I want to thank my cousin Dana for leaving her family to help my mom care for me when I really needed the help. I also want to thank my grandparents and other extended family for their support and prayers.

I want to thank the churches who did so much for me including my home church, East Side Baptist Church as well as Campus Church, Open Bible Baptist Church, Ko'olau Baptist Church, Wilsall Community Church, the school my mom taught at, Thomasville Christian School, and the church connected to the school, Christ Community. I also want to thank the churches in Birmingham, Glen Iris Baptist Church and Mountain View Baptist Church, who reached out and cared for my family and I while we were in Birmingham. I want to thank Jennifer Geesling for all the time she spent helping to care for me. I also want to thank countless other churches and people who prayed for me and supported us.

I want to thank Ellyn Luther for generously giving of her time to edit this book for me. As well as Rachel Grosnick who helped me put the finishing touches on it.

I want to thank Curtis O'Morrow for all his work in designing the book cover.

I want to thank my doctors Jason Lowe, M.D,. Leo Derosier M.D., Rena Stewart M.D., and Barry Callahan, M.D., who did such a great job putting me back together and my therapists and athletic trainers Kim Ingram, Stephen LaPlante, Mary Ball, and Ben Daughtery for getting me moving again! I also want to thank the orthopedic nurses Cherry and Amy who went out of their way to help us and were so kind to my family and I.

Table of Contents

Part One

Tragedy Brings Brokenness

Part Two

Brokenness Brings Beauty

Preface

"Yea, though I walk through the valley of the shadow of death, I will fear no evil: for thou art with me." I guess I never really realized the full meaning of this passage until I actually walked through that valley—a valley that was wrought with the uncertainty of what would be on the other side, endless days of pain and nights of agony, and countless moments of wondering how I would have the strength to make it through the next day. That was the problem-I didn't have the strength. I was in a desperate fight for my life, and I was losing the battle. But God did have the strength, and not only that, He had the rod that comforts, He gave the grace that is sufficient, and He exercised His power as the Great Physician. As I walked through the valley of the shadow of death, my God was with me, and He walked with me every step of the way as I ascended out of that valley. It was a long, rough and, at times, a seemingly impossible valley to climb out of, but my God was faithful. With each painful step that I fought for, His hand was there holding me and guiding me out. It is this story, this struggle, and this blessing from God that I would like to share with you.

I don't really know where to begin. So many people along the way have urged me to write this book and to share about my journey, but quite honestly, it took me a while to really take that urging seriously. It is quite an intimidating task. There are so many things that have happened and so many amazing blessings that it is just impossible to share it all or to even begin to comprehensively convey the gravity behind many of the things that occurred. But I feel that this is the least I can do to show an appreciation first of all to my Savior, who has done so much for me, and also to my family and friends, who were so faithful to support me and lift me up in prayer. I am where I am today because of God's beautiful grace and because of the prayers of God's people.

December 17, 2011—a date that will be forever burned into my memory. While the details of the day may be a bit fuzzy, the effect of that day will be felt for the rest of my life. It was on that day that, in just a split second, my life changed drastically forever. It started out as a fairly typical day. Married for just four months, Michael and I were on vacation for Christmas, and that morning we had celebrated our first Christmas together. We had planned to go to our friends' wedding that evening and then travel to my parents' house for a few days before going to spend a few days with his family. Unfortunately, most of these plans would never come to fruition.

At around 7 o'clock that evening, we left our friends' wedding and headed towards Georgia. At that same time in Troy, Alabama, a girl in her late teens received news that she had gotten a job she had been wanting. She decided to celebrate with some family members, and unfortunately for me, consuming alcohol was involved in that celebration. Around 9:40 p.m., this young girl made a decision to drive home under the influence of alcohol. As our car and her car began to approach each other, on Hwy 231 near Troy, things began to spin out of control. She started to make a turn that was not there, overcorrected, and came barreling across the paved median into our car at a speed somewhere between 88 and 99 mph. In that split second, life as we knew it changed forever. There have been many times that I have thought about that moment. What if we had stayed just a few minutes longer at the wedding or stopped at a gas station for a break? What if we had decided not to go to the wedding, what if she had not gotten that job, or what if she had decided to not try driving? So many scenarios could have changed what happened. But the stark reality that I have come to is that those "what ifs" were not God's plan for my life. Those "what ifs" were not what was best for me. Jeremiah 29:11 states, "For I know the thoughts that I think towards you, saith the Lord, thoughts of peace, and not of evil, to give you an expected end." God explains in this verse that His purpose towards me is never malicious or evil; it is good and meant to bring ultimate peace in my life. Not only that, but He also promises me that what He allows into my life is for a purpose. He has an expected end, or ultimate goal, for my life, and every circumstance He allows into it is meant to bring me to that expected end. You see, many years ago God set out a plan for my life, and in those plans, He included this tragedy. Why, I do not know. I will never fully know or understand during my life here on earth, but what I do know is that He does have a purpose in all of this and that God was, is, and always will be in control. This tragedy could have been prevented if God had chosen to do so, but instead He chose for me to walk through this valley and experience Him in a way few do. My desire and prayer through all of this has been that I will be conformable to God's desires and fulfill my ultimate purpose on this earth of bringing honor and glory to my Savior.

So here's the story. I hope to not be too graphic, but I must provide some details to fully portray what I went through and how my amazing God and His beautiful grace brought me through it.

December 17, 2011: Perhaps the news channel that night stated something like this... "At 9:40 p.m. on Alabama Hwy 231 in Troy, Alabama, a young teenage girl started to make a turn that was not there, overcorrected, and came speeding at 88 to 99 mph into the car of a young newly married couple, resulting in one critically injured and three other injured passengers. It was discovered that the driver responsible for the accident was over the legal limit for alcohol. The driver of the other car was airlifted by Life-Flight to a hospital in Montgomery, Alabama, and is unstable and in critical condition."

Whatever the news and newspapers stated, one thing certain: this was a tragic accident that by all perspectives should have ended in a fatality, but through God's protection, an amazing story of His beautiful grace was about to unfold.

PART ONE

TRAGEDY BRINGS BROKENNESS

CHAPTER 1

December 17, 2011

I never saw it coming. Was it my fault? How did this happen? "Michael, are you okay?" I whispered with as much force as I could. Michael did not budge, so I tried again as loud as I could. "Michael, are you okay?" This time he rolled his head over and moaned some unintelligible words. Then I whispered, "Is Snickers [my puppy] okay?" More unintelligible words. At least he was still responsive. Hopefully, help would be here soon. I was having a lot of trouble breathing, and things were starting to go dark. I looked down and saw a confusing bloody mess, and as the world around me began going dark, I reminded myself that regardless of what happened, I had to stay calm. Then, the darkness surrounded me.

When the rescue personnel arrived, they found a disturbing scene. Two unrecognizable cars rested far apart from each other. The silver Honda Accord, the car that was hit, was in a much worse condition than the other car. A curly blonde head hung out of what used to be the window of the Accord. From all appearances, the young woman looked as if she had not survived the accident, and a decision was promptly made to call for the coroner. As the rescue personnel came to the car to get the man out of the passenger seat, the girl groaned and began trying to talk to the rescue personnel. Because of her responsiveness, her rescuers began to work much more quickly. When they got the passenger side door open, the keys from a keyboard came spilling out onto the pavement. Apparently the passenger had been working on his computer, which would no longer be usable. They worked as quickly as possible to get the passenger, Michael, out. After he was extracted from the car and put in the ambulance, they began frantically working to free the driver. However, it turned out to be a very frustrating task. Because of the location of the impact, the driver had been shoved between the door, the dashboard, and the seat, which had all been crumpled in towards the center of the car. The effects of the impact left very little room for the girl to be squished into and even less room for her to breathe. The rescue personnel noted the extremely shallow breathing of the young girl and knew she would not last long. After running into several complications in trying to free her, they tried to at least release the seat back so she could have more room to breathe. It seemed as if every time they tried to peel the car away from her, she would just come with it. It was as if she was literally part of the car. Finally, when things were looking hopeless and time was running out, the back of the seat sprang back. In that second, the young woman took a deep, full breath and the outlook drastically changed. The rescuers went from thinking the situation might be hopeless to renewed vigor as they realized it was not internal hemorrhaging that was keeping her from taking full breaths. It was just the constricted space she had been in. There was still hope they could save her life!

Forty-five minutes later, they finally extracted the driver from the carnage that was left of the car. As they were pulling her out, the rescue personnel fought to find ways to stabilize her limbs, but because they were broken in so many places, it proved to be difficult. One fireman worked diligently to keep her focused and awake as they attempted to get her stabilized. The Life Flight helicopter landed just as they pulled her out, and they quickly loaded her and began the flight to Baptist Medical Center in Montgomery.

Our car as well as me on the stretcher being wheeled to the helicopter

On arrival at the emergency room, the driver's blood pressure was 60/40 and dropping rapidly, but she was still fighting, talking, and answering questions. She made sure to tell the hospital to call her parents and gave them her parents' number as well as other pertinent medical information. This was an amazing feat with the condition she was in, but of course, anyone who knew her would not be surprised. She has a stubborn, determined streak that is hard to match.

The driver was of course me. That in and of itself is amazing! My family and friends know I hate to drive and rarely do, but on that night, my husband had asked me to drive for just thirty minutes so he could work on a Sunday School lesson for the next day. Again I see God's hand and His grace in this situation. If Michael had been driving, he might not have survived, and four months after being married, I would have been a widow. But God had a different plan in mind, and His hand was about to become more obvious in our lives.

Soon after I arrived at the hospital in Montgomery, tests needed to be run to discover the extent of the damage to my body so appropriate interventions could be implemented. Scans and images needed to be completed to know what brain or spinal cord injuries had taken place. In an accident of this caliber, there had to be some damage, most likely extensive damage. My body was quickly crashing, and I was going to have to be put on life support. The likelihood of my surviving continued to quickly spiral down. Someone needed to contact one of my family members since my husband could not be with me.

They originally transported Michael to the hospital in Troy. Soon after, he was transported to Baptist Medical Center in Montgomery to be in the same hospital as me. Michael was also in quite a bit of pain. His left upper arm was broken, as well as a few ribs and vertebrae, but he was stable. Other than experiencing pain for a while, he would be fine. He would need to recover quickly because of all that he was about to have to face.

Back in Thomasville, Georgia, my parents, Tim and Sharon Robson, and my sister, Charity, were growing concerned. Michael and I should have been home earlier, but we were not answering our phones. My family knew something must be wrong, but nothing could have prepared them for the devastating news the next phone call would bring. At approximately 1:30 a.m., the telephone at their home rang. That phone call was one a parent hopes to never get—a phone call that will turn the world upside down. My mother answered the phone, and the person on the other end from the hospital in Montgomery asked if they could come immediately to the hospital. They were at least three hours away, so she told the man it would take them a while to get there. He asked whether there was anyone closer and of course there was not. He bluntly informed my mom to hurry and get there; they would try to keep me alive as long as they could. The situation was stark. My parents and Charity hurried to gather a change of clothes and what they could think of that they might need and quickly ran out the door. The next three hours were surely the longest three hours of their life. In fact, it probably did not take them the full three hours to get there. What they must have been going through in those hours is unimaginable, wondering if they would even make it before I passed.

At the hospital, doctors had started running their diagnostics, and strangely, there did not appear to be any spinal cord or severe brain damage — truly, an impossibility! Some of the diagnostics were repeated to confirm the original results, and amazingly, God had spared these areas. More impressively, though, there was no internal hemorrhaging. This was a sheer impossibility because of the way the car had been impacted and the way I had been compacted into the side and front of the car. But God had a plan, and those injuries were not in His plan. He protected and preserved those vital areas. However, the imaging did reveal a tremendous amount of musculo-skeletal damage.

Any reader who is squeamish may want to skip the next few paragraphs that describe my injuries in detail. This may be unsettling for some.

Imaging revealed a clearer picture of what was already quite obvious. There were significant injuries, especially to my left side. In several areas, bones had broken and projected out of my skin. In fact, when the rescuers arrived at the scene, my left leg had been crumpled like an accordion and my left thigh bone had exploded out of my leg and was resting straight up by my cheek. My left arm was broken in several places, with bones also piercing through the skin. Imaging showed at least 14 different bones fractured, and many of them were fractured in several different places. My lower left leg as well as the kneecap had been crushed. Dr. Lowe, one of the orthopedic doctors, described it as being like a cracker that someone crushed between their hands. This lower limb appeared unsalvageable, especially with the gaping hole from midshin to ankle where bone, tendons, and muscles were obviously exposed. My left arm was also in bad shape. Both thigh bones had been broken, but thankfully the Lord had spared my right arm. I was going to need that to help with moving around. Several shards of glass were lodged in my eye, and the left side of my face had been sliced open in several places. My left eye bone was also fractured, and it was possible that I might never see out of my left eye again. Most concerning were the images showing a crushed pelvis. The hospital in Montgomery was not equipped to handle this injury, and I would need to be taken to a hospital equipped to deal with this kind of trauma. A phone call was placed to University of Alabama Hospital at Birmingham (UAB), Alabama. Hopefully, they would be willing to care for this injury. Meanwhile, they needed to prep me and get me ready to go to the operating room so they could clean out and stabilize my wounds.

Thankfully, my parents had finally arrived. However, they needed to be warned before going into the room. I was apparently unrecognizable and not doing well. My parents needed to be told that I might not show any signs of recognition. At this point, I was barely clinging to life and over the next few days I would be in a desperate fight for my life.

The doctors and nurses had been right. Lying on the bed, I looked nothing like the Julie my parents knew. I was swollen and bruised and had a tube down my throat breathing for me, and my blonde, curly hair was now red and matted with blood. The left side of my face had several stitches, and my eye, which soon would require the removal of eight shards of glass, was a deep purple and swollen shut. My right hand, with barely discernible fingers due to the swelling, was restrained to the bed to prevent me from pulling out my breathing tube, and my neck was stabilized by a large, uncomfortable brace to prevent movement. Wires, lines, and tubes surrounded my bedside. It was a sobering, complicated scene, straight from their worst nightmare.

So many thoughts and emotions to absorb, but it was not the time to give up. I would need someone to fight for me in the conscious world. With many decisions to be made and many prayers that needed to be prayed, this burden needed to be carried by them for now.

Suddenly, my right hand started moving in an urgent manner. My mom tried to calm me and told me to relax, but I persisted. Eventually, Charity, who was standing by my right hand, realized that I was attempting with my fat, swollen fingers to sign letters. As young children, we both had learned to sign the alphabet and had often used it to communicate when we were not supposed to talk. Everyone began carefully watching my hand as I struggled to communicate. I asked about the accident, whose fault it was, where Michael was, and what was wrong with my legs. My attempt at communication let them know that I did recognize them! Not only that, but I was coherent enough to try to communicate! It was a special blessing and assurance from God. My parents and sister needed to see that I was still fighting and that I needed to understand what was going on. God, in that moment, provided answers for both of those needs.

After the doctors had consulted, they approached my family. The news appeared grim. They needed to take me to surgery immediately, and it appeared that my left leg and possibly my left arm might have to be amputated. The doctors were still anxiously awaiting a call back from UAB. But while they waited, decisions had to be made, and it was time to head to the operating room. On the way down the hall to the OR, the phone call finally came. UAB instructed them to immediately wrap me up and get me on a Life Flight to them. UAB wanted to take care of all the injuries and wanted me there as soon as possible. As quickly as manageable, I was wrapped up, put in the helicopter, and transported to UAB.

Already, word was quickly spreading by Facebook. Many people were fervently seeking the Lord for healing, strength, and wisdom. Tim and Jon (my brothers), currently in Scotland and Africa, respectively, had been contacted and were urgently looking for flights. They hoped to make it sooner rather than later. Christians literally across the world—some who did not even personally know me—were coming together to lift my family and me up to the Great Physician. He was my only hope, and I was in desperate need of His supernatural power.

Facebook Posts:

To help give a clearer, more comprehensive picture of the events that happened, I am including several Facebook posts, journal entries, and pictures.

These first Facebook posts describe in much more detail the events of the first few weeks, since I have no memory of them. Reading these posts will really provide a clearer picture of my story.

Early in the morning, **December 18:**

Charity Robson: "Please pray for my sister, Julie McClure, and her husband. They've been in a serious car accident."

Charity Robson: "Thank you all for the prayers and please continue to pray. Julie is still in critical condition and is going in for surgery at 7:30."

Tim Robson: "My sister goes into surgery in a few minutes. She is listed in critical condition. She has multiple major breaks in both of her legs, her right arm, a cracked shoulder, a cracked hip, extensive vascular damage. Results from CT scan of head and spine have come back with good report. They are hoping to repair as much of this damage to her body as possible in this surgery. Their greatest concern is that she is losing blood and they don't know why. It is possible that the bleeding is linked to all the broken bones and vascular damage. Thank you for all your prayers and support. Please keep praying. These next few hours are critical..."

Charity Robson: "Still waiting for Julie's transfer to UAB...will be a critical transfer so please pray she stays stable 'til she gets there and the surgery will go well. The Lord has protected her brain and she was signing questions and things to mom and me because the breathing tube won't let her talk. She signed "I love you" before I left.....please pray for my big sister!"

Tim Robson: "They have now had to Life Flight Julie to UAB hospital in Birmingham, AL, as her injuries are too extensive for them to deal with in Montgomery. Please pray over the next hour because this transport is critical and she needs to stay stable so they can do surgery when she gets there. They also now have concerns about her lungs because of all the ribs that are broken. Her pelvis is also broken. However, she can move her feet and wiggle her toes. She has come in and out of consciousness. Critical but stable…"

Tim Robson: "It's pretty fantastic that there are people in Ireland, Scotland, England, Turkey, USA, and Canada all praying, thinking, and pulling for Julie and her husband Michael. I pray that they can sense this even now in their spirit. May God use this support from us and power from Him for healing and strength in her body! Thank you all and keep it up!"

On Sunday morning, December 18, I arrived at UAB Hospital. Hospital staff members had to complete all the diagnostics again for their records, and surprisingly, they did not see the crushed pelvis that the Montgomery hospital thought I had. In fact, all they noted were a couple of pelvic fractures that would need no further intervention except to be monitored, but I was in the right place for my other orthopedic injuries to be addressed.

Rapidly getting me into surgery was the highest priority. The longer it took, the worse my outcome would be. Again, doctors reminded my parents that they might have to amputate. They began the long surgery to clean out my wounds and stabilize my bones. They worked on me as long as my body could tolerate. This process would take several surgeries to complete. Because I was young and healthy and did not smoke or drink, the trauma and orthopedic doctors thought it might be possible to save my leg. Eventually, they would place my lower left leg in an Ilizarov external fixator, which consisted of 4 rings attached to 19 pins that were inserted into my bone to hold it in place. This frame could be adjusted to make sure the bone aligned appropriately and would allow for eventual weight-bearing on the leg as it healed. However, in the first few surgeries, the focus was cleaning out the wounds and in some places inserting temporary external fixators to stabilize the broken bones until I was able to tolerate the surgeries to have them internally fixated.

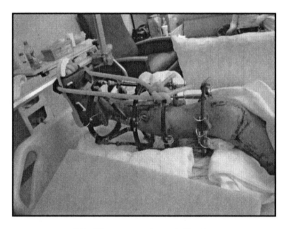

My Ilizarov external fixator

Facebook Posts:

December 19:

Tim Robson: "Julie headed is in for her first actual surgery. Everything up to this point has been prep work. They are attaching metal plates to the outside of her legs to hold the bones in place. As she improves this week, they will do other surgeries to put in pins and rods. In this surgery, they may also repair the break at the top of her right leg. Thanks again for the support and prayer."

Tim Robson: "The list grows of people across the world praying and pulling for

Julie and Michael and our families...Africa, Antigua, Mexico, Guatemala, Scotland, Ireland, England, Turkey, Canada, New Zealand, and Japan...all around the globe! Fantastic! I can feel the prayer and support... What an amazing community of people you are...."

Amy Robson: "Julie has come through the first surgery beautifully. She will be resting today and will then hopefully go back into surgery tomorrow to begin the repair of her left arm. The arm was badly broken—especially her elbow—but the doctor that will be working on her, elbows are her speciality! The doctor today checked her left eye and removed several pieces of glass—don't know at this point if any damage was caused there. But the most AMAZING news is that during the surgery, the doctor was unable to find anything broken in her pelvis!!!! Yes that's right, we had been told that her pelvis had been broken in multiple places. Also, they can now not find any broken ribs. Praise the Lord!! Thank you everyone for prayers—we serve an awesome God!"

Tim Robson: "Pray for my brother Jonathan. He and his family are in Malawi. They are trying to decide if he should come. It is quite the expense to fly from Africa, coupled with the fact of national turbulence, which is a concern for safety of their family. Pray for wisdom and then provision if he does decide to come. He is also having trouble finding a flight that arrives early in the week. Thanks again for all your time in prayer that you are investing in this."

Tim Robson: "Julie is resting tonight. They will take her in for her second round of surgery around 8 a.m. The surgery will last most of the day tomorrow if she stays stable. Thanks for your support and prayers! She is still being responsive and the reports are positive."

Starting that Sunday, a seemingly endless stream of visitors were seen in the waiting room with my family. A church in the area, Glen Iris Baptist Church, brought in meals for the family, and Mountain View Baptist Church members did much to help us out. Lodging was also provided. People who did not know me took time to visit and encourage my family. People traveling for Christmas went out of their way to come by the hospital to offer their support, and some dropped their plans and drove long distances to come support the family. It was amazing to see God's people help shoulder this burden and walk through this tragedy alongside my family.

God also worked in another way. I had always been a "Daddy's girl," and as I could imagine, this was almost unbearable for my dad. However, shortly after my parents arrived at the hospital, my dad had to return to the car to get something out of the trunk. When he opened the trunk, his iPad, without prompting, began playing "God is Faithful" written by Travis L. Boyd and sung by the Sons of Jubal. The words went like this:

"When you find it hard to understand
And you're just not sure you have the strength
To do all God commands
When the task seems overwhelming,
You can rest within His hands.
For the One who called you is faithful!
God is faithful.
He will not forget His own.
God is faithful.

He'll never leave you all alone.

He's right beside you,

Waiting to guide you,

For the one who called you is faithful.

God is faithful!

He is always there when human eyes can't see

So aware of all your hurts and all your deepest needs!

God is faithful!

He will not forget His own.

My God is faithful!

He'll never leave you all alone.

He's right beside you,

Waiting to guide you,

For the One who called you is faithful.

God is faithful!" (Boyd)

It was as if God audibly said to him that things were going to be okay. He was in control. My dad needed that right at that moment! God knew his needs, and as always, He provided.

The next week and a half of my life was a blur for my family and me. I remained sedated on life support and have very few memories at that time, so I will just give a brief summary of what happened and allow the Facebook updates to provide more details of what happened during those days.

During that time, I had to have several more surgeries, none of them shorter than eight hours. The doctors operated each time as long as they could. They were amazed at how well my body tolerated the operations, considering all it had been through. Basically, every other day had another major surgery. The biggest concern the doctors had at that time was infection. With my weakened immune system and open areas on my skin, I was at very high risk. I had some trouble with my lungs, and a procedure had to be done to help my breathing. The Facebook updates don't include this, but on December 23, the doctors told my parents that they needed to get me off the ventilator (life support) by the 27th because of the potential for a lung infection. If they could not get me off, they would have to put in a tracheostomy. Of course, that was not something Michael or my parents wanted, and they had many people praying that I could wean off the ventilator. They tried once on the 23rd and were not successful. Apparently, according to my family, I showed my stubbornness again during this time, being persistent with the nurses about getting the tube out and getting my neck brace off. I even tried to convince my sister to untie my right hand so I could remove the tube myself. But I couldn't convince her, and I gave her an angry stare. Finally, on December 25, Christmas Day, I was able to start breathing on my own, and that is the point my memories begin.

Michael's Journal Entry:

December 25: Julie was taken off from anesthesia and told me that she loved me! This is the day that God gave me back my beautiful wife Julie! Praise God. Direct answer to my specific prayer!

Facebook Posts:

December 20:

Tim Robson: "As Julie has been signing to us with her right hand (she is left-handed), she expressed concern for Michael, her job, and her injuries. She was really happy to see me and hoped Amy and the kids were here, but I told her they couldn't make it. She also told us "I love it here." She is quite a skilled nurse so she also has asked us many times to describe her injuries."

Tim Robson: "Julie has now gone into surgery. We told her that people from all over the world are praying for her. She smiled really big and spelled out in sign language letters... "That's Cool. Keep praying. It hurts." She can't talk because of all the tubes, but when she is not under, she is alert and trying to sign to us. The surgery will last for hours. Pray for her doctors and her nurses and of course strength for her."

Tim Robson: "It pains us to see her this way, but God has been good to us and she is alive. We are so blessed to have family and friends like you. So many of you have cared for us. From food and motel expenses to recommendations and connections for legal care and representation, many already have stopped by to visit and sit with us. When we told Julie about this she signed "so cool." Thank you guys. We need it."

Tim Robson: "Just heard from the doctors... They are finished with the femur on her right leg which was completely broken in half. She is stable. They are moving on to the left arm. Now they are repairing the ulna and the radius of her left arm, which were both broken in half. If she is still stable, they will deal with her left elbow, which was completely shattered."

Tim Robson: "Julie is done with today's surgery. She is stable. They are cleaning her wounds and moving her back into her ICU room. They finished her lower and upper left arm. Dr. Stewart was very happy with her condition today and confident of how the surgery turned out. They are saving the complex elbow surgery till Jan. 2 so as to let the swelling go down. There is no other doctor in the country that could do this complex surgery that Julie needs. Amazingly, she is based here at UAB! Tomorrow will be a day of rest. Thursday, they hope to clean the wounds again. Monday, they hope to do the major surgery on her left leg where the worst of her injuries are. This will likely be an all-day event. You guys are amazing! The support you have shown today and the prayers you have prayed have sustained Julie and us today. Keep it up!"

Tim Robson: "Everyone is settling in for the night. Julie is sleeping well and continues to be stable. They are possibly needing to give her fluids and blood because her levels are a little low. We got to see her for an hour. She is very swollen but this should go away in a day or so. Mom is sleeping from 9 to 3 while Dad is with Julie. Then dad will sleep from 3 to 9 while Mom is with Julie. They are very strong today but at times showed signs of strain and weariness. They have only slept a few hours since Sunday. We hope to talk them into taking a nap tomorrow. We are all hurting but I can tell they are deeply affected by this. They are also overwhelmed by the support all have shown. Several times today they were in tears as the realized the generosity and care that has been shown to us these past days. Please pray for

Julie to have a good night of rest and the same for all day tomorrow. Pray for no infection and accelerated healing of her repaired bones and wounds."

December 21:

Tim Robson: "Good morning everyone! Julie rested well and had a good night! Mom and Dad were both able to get some sleep as well. We have high hopes that Michael and his family will arrive today. We are still working on details and trying to figure out lodging for the next few weeks."

Tim Robson: "The nurses just came and told us that they were going to take a look at Julie's lungs with a scope. Her oxygen levels have been a little low and there is some fluid. Also they were not happy with her chest X-rays so they wanted to take a look. Again, pray for protection against infection and now especially pneumonia. Thank you guys for your vigilance and standing with us for Julie. Here we go with another day of making a difference for Julie!"

Tim Robson: "Julie is resting well today. Levels have been great, and her swelling is going down quickly. The scope for her lungs went well. They where able to drain a bit of fluid, and there was nothing in her lower lungs. They also started her on some nutrients, which is great! Also, they have moved her to 8-hr increments for all her checkups and tests. She is doing really great! Thank you guys for praying. Michael should be on his way over today! This will be so needed for the 2 of them to reunite!"

Tim Robson: "Michael is finally here! Pray for him and his family as right now they are heading to see Julie for the first time since the accident."

December 22:

Tim Robson: "Good morning everyone! Julie is still resting this morning. She had a really good night. All levels are great, her swelling has gone way down, and she has some lovely color in her face! She is not going into surgery today. They have decided to do the major left leg surgery tomorrow. This will be a 12- to 15-hr. surgery depending on how stable she is. They hope to repair both the upper and lower leg and knee injuries. Today she will rest and they are trying to wean her off the breathing tube a bit today. The desire is for her to come off the tube next Thursday. If she doesn't come off by then, she will have to have a tracheotomy. After two weeks of a breathing tube, there is high risk of pneumonia. The doctors are really positive about how Julie has responded to everything and feel she will be off of the tube by when she needs to be. The optometrist came by this morning and says her eyes look great! Thank you again for the day-by- day support and prayers. Most moments we feel overwhelmed and completely surrounded by the goodness of God through you!"

Tim Robson: Please pray for Julie to rest and have a solid day of recovering her strength for the all-day surgery tomorrow. Pray for wisdom for the doctor and nurses as they are still consulting about how to deal with Julie's left leg injuries tomorrow. Pray for their skill and for them to be able to rest before the surgery. Pray for Julie's lung strength so she can come off the respirator assistance. Please pray for Mom and Dad. All of this is setting in on them pretty hard today... Dad especially. He is really worried about the upcoming surgeries and he is exhausted. We are trying to get them to rest but they are so committed to being with Julie. Pray for just a huge dose of the Holy Spirit to come and comfort them and provide them with rest and strength that goes beyond sleep. Also pray for their strength to double as they sleep."

Tim Robson: "Prayer for Michael... He has a broken left arm that needs healing. His lungs were injured and he is having trouble breathing. He has some cracks in a few of his vertebrae and this is causing him much pain. As he is recovering, he is also wrestling with this reality of Julie's condition and the long-term effects of these injuries. Pray for rest for him so he can have an awareness of all the details that he needs to attend to. Pray for wisdom with all the details that he will need to make decisions about."

December 23:

Tim Robson: "Good morning friends... Julie has gone into surgery. It will just be a long day of waiting for the phone to ring every 2 hrs. to get a report. Doctors were positive this morning and said they will go as long as she can tolerate. Looks like 10 hrs-plus of surgery. Julie was raising her arm and making faces this morning! She also was trying to take her breathing tube out! She does not like that thing! All this while sedated! Pray for the doctors' skill, creativity, and endurance today! Pray for stability and strength for Julie while the surgery is going on so the doctors can get her whole left leg done."

Tim Robson: "Just received an update on Julie... femur is done! Tibia is done! On to the obliterated knee cap... They said she is doing fabulous! Here we grow... Wow! What a job you have done on her behalf... Thank you, Thank you, Thank you!"

Tim Robson: "We just met with Julie's surgeon. He gave us a great report. The left leg is done for 6-8 weeks. He put a cement antibiotic spacer in to help the upper bone to align and begin to heal. He put something similar to a halo on her lower leg for the two major breaks which allows them to draw the bones into place and make adjustments over the next few days. This allowed them to do the operation without major incisions to the lower leg. The knee cap is a concern because half of it is missing. This will very likely lead to arthritis, joint slippage, and displacement. Overall, Mission 1 accomplished! Julie's leg is back together! Mission 2! The major concern now is the healing of the open wounds. She has major open

37

wounds on the upper, middle, and lower parts of her leg. The lower leg has an area 7 cm by 11 cm uncovered by skin. There is a long "s" wound from her midthigh to the middle of her shin. He was serious about this being the most dangerous part of this whole recovery section. If there was infection, first they would operate to remove it. The worst case would be amputation, which he says is a possibility but at this point not the focus. The other concern is bone death and infection. Some of the breaks were so extensive that the bone still there is stripped and damaged. The surgeon said, "Here are our 3 things to focus on: Skin rejuvenation, protection from infection, and rehab!"

December 24:

Tim Robson: "Good morning to our growing community that has gathered around Julie! She is awake today! We all have been in to speak to her. She is groggy but is smiling and nodding. She keeps trying to sign letters but we make her relax. She was very happy to see Michael and to hear that we are going to rent *White Christmas* for us to watch together today at some point. We have been reading her cards to her, and the nurses of the unit put together a big poster for her! Thank you all for everything! We are breathing a bit lighter now that she is awake! This morning we spoke with the doctors, and after viewing the new x-rays of her leg they are very pleased. Again one of the doctors told us "pray against infection" so that's the key! Today should be a quiet day of rest! I will update you if we find out anything else!"

Tim Robson: "A great day with Julie! She was awake most of the day. She is starting to be in pain because they have cut the propofol back. We decorated her room with glittery Christmas ornaments and lights! However, she was not happy with the lights! They most likely hurt her eyes. We sang Christmas carols as we decorated and made lighthearted jokes to make her smile. The doctors have moved her back to just pressure support and hope to take the tube out tomorrow! Yeah

38

baby! She is quite anxious to have it out. She kept biting it and moving her nose cause she doesn't like it. Well we are off to see her for an hour and then to get some rest."

December 25:

Tim Robson: "Merry Christmas everyone! And a Merry day it is indeed. Julie is awake and very much keeping us in line. The breathing tube should come out in about an hour! Hope you all have a lovely day with your families!"

Charity Robson: "Merry Christmas to everyone! We are thanking the Lord for answered prayer. I asked the Lord specifically to allow her to have her tube out on Christmas. Doctors have just taken it out and I'm about to have the first face-to-face conversation with my sweet sister since August. Praise our Almighty Father for His goodness!"

CHAPTER 2

Waking Up

"*W*here am I? Why am I hurting so bad?" I looked up and I saw a nurse. She turned to some other people and told them they needed to get me to the hospital. I watched as a helicopter landed nearby. They quickly loaded me and took me to a hospital. At the hospital, the doctor came in and told me I was pregnant and that they could save my baby if I could just stay alive for 24 hours. I was in so much pain that I had difficulty breathing. I had no idea whether I could make it that long, but for this baby I was going to try.

I was wheeled into the center of what looked like a white dome. The doctor referred to it as an incubator. This would help prepare my baby to be ready for birth. This was where I would spend the next 24 hours trying to hang on to life. My husband, Michael, was there with me encouraging me to hang on. There were so many emotions rushing through my head—frustration, anger, helplessness, fear, and determination to stay alive. It seemed like forever that I lay in there in absolute agony trying to survive. Finally, the time was up, and they told me it was time for them to take the baby.

The next thing I remember is waking up staring at a blue sheet that was hung down to prevent me from seeing my stomach. Michael was standing by my bed with a smile, and I heard a faint cry in the background. I looked over at Michael, who told me that the baby had made it and that she was going to be fine. They just needed to take her to the nursery for a few hours. The relief and joy that flooded over me were unexplainable, and I slowly drifted back to sleep.

I woke up in a hospital room, still in quite a bit of pain but relieved that the worst was over. Michael was standing beside me with his left arm in a cast and holding our little girl. He came closer to my bedside so I could see her and said, "Here's our Layla." She was beautiful. She had a lot of brown hair and was peacefully sleeping, curled up in Michael's arms. My parents and sister were also in the room. The room was small, with noises that ranged from quiet beeps to methodic clicking, as the IV pumps worked to push the needed fluids. I lay there staring at Layla until I drifted off to sleep again.

This scene happened several times until one time I woke up and something was different.

It must be Christmas, I thought. As I looked around, there were several small Christmas decorations scattered around the room. My mind was in a fog. It felt almost like I was dreaming. My family had exhausted, yet happy expressions. My dad had just started praying. I listened as he thanked the Lord for His blessings and for sending His Son so we had something to celebrate that day. He also thanked the Lord for the extra special gift He had given them that day and what a blessing it was to have her. Of course, I thought he was talking about Layla, but I was soon to find out that was not the case.

I looked over at Michael, and something was missing. "Where's Layla?" I asked him. He looked at me with a puzzled expression and asked, "Who's Layla?"

How could he not know? The look of shock on his face was confusing. "Our baby," I said. He promptly responded, "We don't have a baby." As I looked around, my family all had looks of concern and confusion on their face. They all confirmed what Michael had said.

It was like a bombshell. Why did he say, "we don't have a baby"? I had seen her. We had named her. He had been holding her. Had something happened? Were they protecting me from something? Why would they lie to me? I didn't want to be protected; I wanted to know the truth. Confusion, pain, and frustration surrounded me as I drifted off to sleep.

The next few days are a blur. I have brief memories of friends and coworkers who came to visit. I told them stories of what had happened, intermingling true details with details from my dream. My mind still had not come to grips with the true reality, and I struggled to distinguish reality from dream. Often as I lay there, I wondered whether my family was covering up the truth about my baby so that I wouldn't have to deal with it right then. It seemed so real. How could it not be true?

One night when I was alone with my mom, I asked her, "Did I really not have a baby?" She calmly explained how and why that was an impossibility. As I lay there and thought about it, reality finally came into focus. It was all a dream—a very, very real dream, but nonetheless a dream. First, relief washed over me as I realized I would not have to care for a child and miss out on many things because of the recovery I faced. But this realization was quickly followed by a wave of sadness. That child was real to me. To this day,

I can still picture her sweet face. I can clearly see Michael holding her as she slept. She was my baby girl that I had fought for, that I had stayed alive for so that she could have life. Now she was gone. In reality, she had never truly existed. It was a complicated emotion saying good-bye to someone who meant so much yet had never really existed. How could I explain that to someone who hasn't lived that experience without sounding crazy? It was impossible. It was a sadness I would have to deal with on my own time, a sadness that I spent many nights crying over until I eventually accepted it. Right then, I needed to focus on the long, hard recovery ahead of me. It was time to put everything I had into it.

Facebook Posts:

December 26:

Tim Robson: "Well today has just been a day of sitting around and chatting with our Julie. She was fully aware and awake and may even get to have dinner tonight if she feels up to it! Tomorrow she has an angiogram to prepare for a "flap" of skin to be taken from her back and grafted into the gaping wound on her left leg. So far infection free! Wow! We are so thankful for your prayers and support. The days ahead are full of challenges for Julie, but we will face them together with faith and promise!"

December 27: I was finally getting out of the ICU! I was going to have a room where we could actually close the door, have a little more space, and all be together all the time. This was great news! I was determined to ask the doctor for a bed with a trapeze bar on it in the new room. The trapeze set attached to and went over the bed with a triangular handhold that dropped down to allow patients to use it to pull up. I knew it would be a big help. While I was in the ICU, some of the staff had roughly and carelessly attempted to put me on a full-size bedpan, regardless of my request for them to find a fracture bedpan, which is half the size. The incident had resulted in indescribable pain that took quite some time to get under control. I was not about to let that happen again and would do anything I could to prevent it. At least with the trapeze set, I could help some by pulling up on the bar with my right arm, and I could use it to help shift my weight to prevent bed sores. With two broken thigh bones, two knees that were not supposed to bend, and a heavy circular external fixator on my left lower leg, turning or moving, in general, was a near impossibility.

Finally, we arrived in my own room. I was exhausted from the move and hurting badly. Apparently, from the conversations I kept overhearing, I had a pretty big surgery coming up soon. At least I would be put to sleep and wouldn't feel the pain for a while.

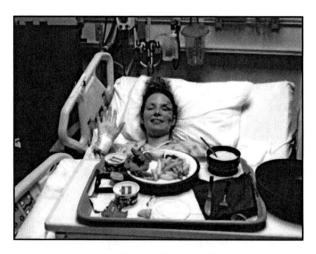

Eating my first meal!

44

I looked up to see my plastic surgeon, Dr. Derosier, walk through the door. I could tell he had a lot on his mind and seemed to be deliberating some major decisions. He came to me and introduced himself. I was sure I had met him before but did not have any recollection of him. He was kind and kept my family very well informed. He made an impressive first impression. He pulled out his magic marker and began drawing on my leg as he explained to me that for the gash in my leg, they were going to need to take some muscle. He contemplated using muscles from my thigh, but as he kept on drawing, he confirmed what he had previously thought. There was not a big enough area of undamaged muscle for them to take on either leg. He then explained to me what must have previously occupied his mind: he needed to decide which muscle to take for the graft. Well, I may have been quite sedated on a lot of medication, but when he told me this, my sense of humor decided to come out. As he walked out the door, I said, "Doctor, just take it from my butt. I have plenty there!" The comment may have surprised him some until he turned and saw the smile on my face. He then proceeded to tell me why that would be a bad decision, but I still thought it was funny. I have always been teased for being very blessed in that area and what better way to get rid of it! At least in my mind, ever since that moment, we have been friends. My surgeons were my heroes, and in my opinion, I had some of the best!

Facebook Posts

December 27:

Charity Robson: "I loooooooove sister time! Just spent 2 hours with my sis telling her a story and chatting.....I will never take these times for granted again.... even if it is in the hospital! Thank You Lord for being with my sister."

December 28:

Tim Robson: "Julie had a restful day where we all got to hang out with her a lot! Lots of friends came by for visits on this beautifully sunny day. Thanks again today for your prayers and the warm connections through being together with Julie. Tomorrow Julie will go to surgery to repair the gaping wound on her left leg. They will take a flap of skin and a piece of muscle from her stomach area and graft it to the wound. Then she will need her leg suspended in traction for 5 days. This surgery should take 6-8 hrs. Please pray for her stability and freedom from infection. Pray for endurance and a sharpness for her doctors as this is a tedious surgery. Pray for encouragement and high spirits, for she is not excited about having her leg in traction. Thanks again for your faithful prayers and support as we move into week 2 of Julie's recovery!"

December 28: I needed sleep! The surgery in the morning would be a long one and an important one for saving my leg, but sleep evaded me. As I lay uncomfortably in the hospital bed thinking, I was amazed at the absolute peace that surrounded me. My body was in total turmoil. I was physically broken, literally shattered to pieces in more than one place. I did not know whether I could keep my leg, I was in extreme pain, but emotionally I was at peace. I spent a few minutes praying, trying to understand things, and I felt this over-whelming comfort come over me. This was God's plan. He had a bigger purpose in it. My plea at this time was not "God, why me???" Rather, it was "God, why did you choose me? What is it you want to accomplish through me?" God gave my mind peace about it all, and I needed to share it with someone.

"Mom."

She quickly got up from her chair where she would spend the night and came to my bedside.

"I just want you to know that I am okay with all of this. I know this was not my plan for my life this semester, but I know this is God's plan. I would rather be in His will than any other place."

I meant every word of it because God had given me the peace that passes all understanding. I knew He had allowed me to be physically broken, but I also knew He had enabled me to accept it and was giving me strength to fight this battle.

The rest of that night was full of crazy, vivid dreams. I woke up several times, urgently telling my mom that we had to tell them about the colored super-hero Rice Krispies treats. I am not sure whom we were supposed to tell and why I thought it was so urgent and such a great idea, but each time I woke up, Mom would just calmly tell me that we would tell them in the morning. It was a long night for both of us.

Up until this surgery, I had what they called a Wound V.A.C. filling the gash in my leg, promoting healing and protecting the open area of my leg from infection. The dressing for the Wound V.A.C. included foam used to fill the wound and a clear adhesive over the top holding it in place. At about 5 a.m. on the morning of December

29th, while barely awake, I saw someone working with my Wound V.A.C. Suddenly, there was a sharp, ripping pain all down my lower left leg. There goes my Wound V.A.C. dressing, I thought. Anger and frustration do not even begin to describe what I felt. I know that I may have appeared to be "out of it" because of the medication, but I was still very aware of what was going on not to mention definitely feeling everything. A warning would have been greatly appreciated, but at least it was over. Now it was time for the longest and most important surgery of my recovery.

For the next 12 hours, my body underwent an intense operation as the doctors removed part of my abdominal muscle and a layer of skin from the left side of my thigh and prepared them to be placed in the lower part of my leg. My doctor spent hours looking through a microscopic lens as he expertly stitched the skin and muscle in place through the bars and pins of my external fixator. Finally, a very exhausted plastic surgeon walked out of the OR to report a successful surgery to my family. The next few days were crucial as we would wait to see whether the graft, or "flap," would take. The area would need to be closely monitored.

Facebook Posts:

December 29:

Tim Robson: "Well, after 12 hours of surgery starting at 9:30 a.m. this morning Julie is back in a room. She is in a lot of pain and still groggy from her surgery. Her left leg is suspended in traction to give the graft the optimal position to take, grow, and begin to regenerate skin in the area of the wound. The doctors are pleased with her surgery. This is the most pivotal time for her to remain free from infection. We will also try to entertain her to keep her mind off of the pain and not being able to move. Please pray for protection from infection, peace of mind, and multiplication of strength to deal with the pain. Thank you for your amazing prayers, words, food, and visits. It has helped sustain us in this time."

"Wow! When he said it would look like a sirloin was on my leg, he wasn't kidding!" That was my thought as I looked at my leg, which was suspended up in the air. The flap was huge and red with a crazy mesh of skin lying over it. My leg would have to stay above my heart level for about three months for the majority of the time to protect the viability of the flap. My plastic surgeon had explained the importance of this, warned me about the size of my flap at first, and informed me that with time, it would shrink. I was glad for the warning, because even with it, the size of my flap was still a shock!

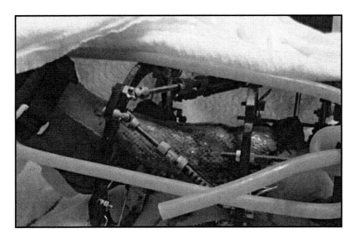

My flap (muscle-skin graft).

Nurses were in and out of my room frequently to check the status of my flap, my pulse, and the color of the flap and the surrounding areas. The plastic surgeon was very happy with how my flap looked. Each time he walked in the room, he would exclaim that it looked great! However, that was not how I would have chosen to describe it. Most of the time, we kept it covered because of how gruesome it looked, but I guess that is a matter of perspective. Most people had to step out of the room when they looked at the flap. It definitely took some getting used to. My plastic surgeon must have known I was struggling with it. He told me that every time I struggled with my flap, I should look at my toes and remember that if it weren't for the flap, then my toes wouldn't be there. There have been many times that I have had to remind myself of that. I may have a severely scarred and disfigured leg, but I do still have my leg, and that is something to be thankful for!

After my flap surgery, I enjoyed a few days' break before the next surgery. I was, however, frequently reminded that one of my abdominal muscles had been removed. Each time I tried to move in any direction, I felt an extreme soreness. At times, this soreness made it difficult even to breathe! Thankfully, the severe soreness faded in just a couple of days!

Facebook Posts:

December 30:

Tim Robson: "Good morning everyone... Julie is doing great. She is awake but very, very tired. She has had lots of visitors today, which she has really enjoyed. Some of the girlfriends brought Dad Krispy Kreme so he is happy! She is in a big room so we get to hang out with her a lot! There is still a lot of pain, but it has been wonderful how strong she has been so far."

December 31:

Tim Robson: "Well it is midday here and all is well. Julie is resting and a bunch of us are hanging out in her room. This room has windows on two sides so the blue skies are visible and the sunshine pours in! The doctors are happy with the flap procedure and the progression so far! It's good to see the swelling going down from her left leg. It is looking better each day! Continued thanks to the lovely people from Glen Iris Baptist Church and Mountain View Baptist for their continued provision of yummies for our tummies in these long days! Special thanks to the Robertsons for the gift certificate to "Siren," a Thai restaurant which fed us and a group of friends that were here! We are waiting to hear about the last surgery for Julie's elbow, which will take place hopefully Monday. Thanks again for all that each of you have poured into our lives and into Julie and Michael!"

January 1:

Tim Robson: "As lovely a day as it could be... Sun was shining, had a wee sing-along and thought from dad (which Julie managed to stay awake through!). We took some time to share encouragements and thoughts with each other ending with some time of prayer for Julie. There were a lot of laughs and tears! Dad Skyped with East Side Baptist Church this morning, where he was projected on the big screen... That was a lot of Preacher up there! Rich and Sara Williams and their girls are here for a visit. They treated us to a meal at KFC, which made Dad very happy! He said this almost feels like a normal Sunday, so he went and took a wee nap! Last night Julie made it to 12 a.m. EST and brought in the new year with a game of Taboo! This morning was a bit rough for Julie because they changed her sheets, which ended up causing her a lot of pain. We have spent the rest of the afternoon watching football and eating Sara's peanut butter balls! Thank you for all that you have shared with our family in 2011. Happy New Year and may you share in the experience of a loving, caring family that we have had because of you!"

Tim Robson: "As far as we know, Julie will go into surgery around 7:30 a.m. and it should last 4-6 hrs. They will be reconstructing her shattered elbow. This will hopefully be the last one for a while! The doctors are really happy with the flap. So far, no infection and it seems to be grafting perfectly. The doctor told Dad this morning, "That is one amazing young lady." My dad told him, "Her faith in the Amazing God sustains her." Julie told Dad yesterday that she was at peace with what has happened to her. She says she trusts that if God chose this for her, He knew that she could handle this and whatever comes with this with His help. With some of the financial struggles that are ahead for Julie and Michael, Charity said that God didn't bring her through a life-threatening car crash to have them overcome by financial difficulty! Again, thanks for your prayers, which have helped keep our faith strong!"

During the few days off from surgery, I enjoyed seeing several of my close friends who had come to visit. It meant the world to me to have such great friends there supporting me through those tough days. New Year's Day came and went, and now it was time to head back to the OR. My elbow had been severely damaged in the wreck and would have to be reconstructed. The surgery had been attempted once, but my body was unable to tolerate it. Hopefully, this time would be different.

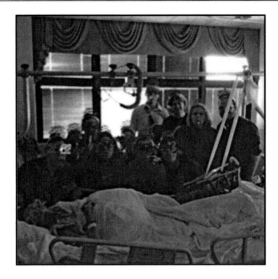

Celebrating New Year's with some friends!

January 2: I underwent my elbow surgery. It would be my last major surgery for a few months. I remember being upset about having surgery that day because my favorite college team, the Georgia Bulldogs, were playing their bowl game that day. I joked with the workers in pre-op about how disappointed I was to miss the game, and the minute I woke up in post-op, that was the first thing I asked about. They all thought it was humorous that I was so concerned about the game and had fun teasing me when the Bulldogs lost.

Dr. Stewart, my elbow surgeon, was an upbeat, enthusiastic doctor and had been an encouragement to my family all along. She was great at keeping them informed and giving them hope through the situation. She informed them that the surgery had gone as planned and that I would need to start moving my elbow after 48 hours. I was taken back to my room for the night. However, that night after the surgery was a miserable night.

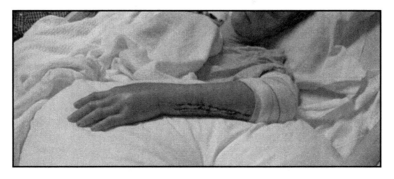

Recovering after elbow surgery

Facebook Posts:

January 2:

Tim Robson: "Julie was in surgery from 9:25 to 3:30 and then wrap-up for another 2 1/2 hrs. The surgeon was extremely happy with the whole procedure. Below the elbow they put in screws and plates to put the bone back together. The upper elbow is where the most severe damage was. There is a significant amount of bone missing. They did the same procedure as with her upper left leg. They inserted a cement spacer that is loaded with antibiotics. In 6-10 weeks, they will need to do a bone graft surgery once most of these wounds have healed. Dr. Stewart says that Julie will need to start gently bending her elbow in 48 hrs. She said when we offer her chicken from Chick-fil-A that we just hold it a bit out of reach. Julie has been a bit groggy and in pain. They put her back in the bigger room in the plastic surgery unit so we can all hang out with her! She managed to watch a little football for a bit and have some conversation with us. So we are finally done with the major surgeries! Thank you, God! Now we need major healing, grace for pain, strength for recovery, and protection from infection. Soon we will be having discussions about what's next and the rehab process... Crazy, huh?! May you all have a blessed night and have an abundant return for what you have given and shared with us!"

I jarred awake and slammed on my pain pump button as hard as I could. The searing pain down my arm was almost unbearable! What was going on?!? I waited a few minutes to see whether the pain medication would kick in, but it never did. For the next hour, I stared at the clock and counted down the 15 minutes between each time I could push the pain pump button, hoping with each push that the pain would diminish, but nothing was happening. It felt like someone was holding my left arm over a fire and just letting it roast. I groaned as tears streamed down my face. This was unbearable! I needed something different to treat this pain. I had always heard nerve pain was awful and basically untouchable by narcotics. Well, now I was experiencing that firsthand. I lay awake most of the night waiting for the doctors to make their rounds. I was desperately hoping my surgeon would give me something different for this nerve pain. Finally, 5 a.m. arrived and Dr. Stewart walked into the room. I am sure she knew immediately that I was not doing well. I told her what I had felt all that night and asked her for something that would help nerve pain. Thankfully, she started me on Neurontin, which, after several days and several dose adjustments, did get my nerve pain under control.

Each day after my elbow surgery, I became more and more aware of what was going on. I slept a lot but enjoyed visits from several friends, old and new. The nurses that took care of me were often fed and serenaded by all of my visitors.

Now that I was more alert and my pain was better controlled, it was time to address my hair. Blood had remained matted in my hair for the last few weeks because I just hadn't had the strength to deal with my hair being yanked on as we attempted to get the clumped blood out. This process would take several days—Mom washed it with a special shower hat the hospital had and then, as gently as possible, brushed out just a section each day. I would have loved to just chop it all off, but Michael would have been sad, so we patiently worked through each piece until we finally got it all combed out!

The doctor who had removed the shards of glass from my eye also came by my room during that time. He did a few eye exams and then looked at me—shocked. He informed my family and me that as far as he could tell from the limited exam he could do in the hospital room, I had no damage to my eyesight! This was another huge answer to our prayers!

These days were not without their complications, though. We ran into pain pumps not working, urinary tract infections and, perhaps the most concerning complication, a large hematoma that had developed on my abdomen where my muscle had been removed. Dr. Derosier, my plastic surgeon, was very concerned with this development. Initially, he wanted to take me to surgery immediately, but after some serious deliberating on his part and begging on my part, he decided he would give it one day to improve. I really did not want to go back to surgery. Tremendous exhaustion had set in, and I just did not feel like I could handle another surgery. Thankfully, the next morning the hematoma had significantly improved, and the plastic surgeon and I both breathed a sigh of relief. He joked with me for causing him to lose a night's sleep worrying over the decision he had made, but he was not the only one who had lost sleep over it!

During these days, as I lay in my hospital bed, I could not help but be thankful for my faith. Each day, we placed on the marker board in my room an encouraging verse. These verses constantly provided encouragement and often challenged me to keep fighting. Each day, my family was provided with food and encouragement from people they did not even know who were brothers and sisters in our faith. Each day, I was provided with love and support from believers around the world. How amazing to see the family of God not just feeling sorry for me for having to go through this but actually coming alongside my family and me and walking through this journey with us. Sharing the burden truly made it more bearable.

January 6: This was the day that my brother Tim was scheduled to return to Scotland. This really upset me because Jon had already had to leave and they had been such a help to have around. Tim had been great with helping me and with keeping everyone calm. I had begged him to stay for a little while longer, at least until we went home from the hospital. He walked into the room that morning as if he was getting ready to leave. Then, he finally decided to tell me he was going to stay. Tears of joy streamed down my face. I still remember how glad and relieved I was that he was staying.

Also that day, I met my trauma surgeon for the first time—at least for the first time that I can remember. She had several fellows with her, and I could hear her quickly relaying my history to them. She walked into the room, looked at me, and said that in the next few days we needed to think about getting me out of bed into a wheelchair.

"In the next few days? I am so tired of this bed," I thought, as she continued to tell me why it was important. I looked at her and said, "I want to get in the wheelchair today."

A look of surprise crossed her face, and she broke into a smile and said, "Okay, she wants to get up today! Let's make sure it happens!"

I knew getting up would be a process and most likely a very uncomfortable one, but it was time to get serious about getting up. It would be just the beginning of a very long road to recovery.

Facebook Posts:

January 6:

Tim Robson: "Hello everyone! Had a nice day with Julie today! She was really awake and for the most part comfortable. Some of the pain she was experiencing was not relieved by the normal meds so she asked for something to relieve nerve pain. In the surgery that was done on her left elbow area, the surgeon had to move the nerve over and then move it back. She told us that this would cause discomfort and some numbness for a number of days after the surgery. Also, Julie's left hand has been really swollen since the operation so the tightness causes real irritation. Her self-administrating pain pump was causing her left arm to hurt really bad so they took her off that and gave her different dosages of pills. The combination of the nerve pain pills and the new dosages have really helped to curb the pain and help it be bearable. Her heart rate was pretty high yesterday and she didn't feel too great. We realized the wound drains in her abdomen have been bleeding some so they gave her another unit of blood and she is doing much better. She has been doing physical therapy every day on the parts she can move, and you can tell she is very determined. Mom has been great about helping her to remember which exercises she needs to do and when they need to happen! Tomorrow they have to change her bed linens, which is usually very painful but we think it will be good for her to move. They also hope to get her into a wheelchair for a ride and to sit up a bit! We were encouraged by visits from friends from Birmingham, Thomasville, and Pensacola. We also got the news that they might be sending us home Tuesday or Wednesday! This is exciting, but we also are starting to think logistically regarding Julie's long-term care. Pray for wisdom and the right connections with the right physical therapist and personal care nurses! Also pray for Mom, Dad, and Michael as they begin to do most of the care. Michael sees the doctor tomorrow about his arm. We are hoping he gets the cast off and gets a new device with a joint. This device would also be removable so he could take a shower. This is necessary... trust me! He has been assisting mom with every need that Julie has. He has also sat for hours at a time reading the lovely notes and encouraging words that you have sent this way! Continue to pray for healing, protection from infection, and wisdom for all the details that still need to be sorted. Thanks again for sticking with us with your prayer and support! May the peace of Christ go with you…"

Finally, around 3 p.m., the therapist walked into the room, dragging along a hoyer lift. It would be my only transportation out of the bed for the next two months. The therapist had to take quite a bit of time to explain the lift to my family, since they would have to do this on their own once we left the hospital. However, the one we got to take home was not quite as fancy as the hospital one. Ours required quite a bit more physical labor! It made for some great memories though! As the therapist finished explaining how the lift worked, she turned to me and told me that it would probably be uncomfortable and that I might not be able to go all the way to the chair. If I needed to stop and go back, I should not feel bad. For the hoyer lift to work, they first would have to get the sling under me that would support my weight. To me, this was the worst part, as it required a lot of turning, which resulted in significant pain. But once it was under me, they just had to hook it up and hand me the remote, and the rest was up to me.

As I thought through this hoyer lift process and thought about my knees that could not bend and the large ex-fix on my left leg, I realized that this was not going to work without help. I would need someone to support each leg while I transferred. After I figured this out, it was finally time to try it. I had the remote in my hand, and I was anxious but excited to get out of the bed. I began pushing the button and I started moving up from the bed! I was still anxious about my legs, but this was kind of fun! I went up and then swung over the side of the bed to the chair that was by the bed and lowered myself down! It was great! It didn't hurt too bad, and I loved finally being out of the bed!

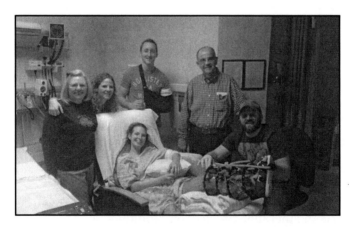

First time up out of bed!

Since it was my first time getting up, I did not stay up for long, but I hated having to get back in the bed. I could not wait until the next day when I could get up again, hopefully for a little longer. Maybe if I was really nice to the nurses, they would let me go out in the sun for a few minutes!

My wish was granted! The next day had come, and I was going to go on a trip around the hospital and then go outside for just a few minutes. It was the beginning of January and pretty cold out, so I would not stay out long, but just a few minutes of fresh air would be amazing! We made the trip downstairs and parked in front of a large window near one of the hospital entrances. It was fun to people-watch and to enjoy the fellowship of several visitors who had come to see me. We took our time and even ate lunch while we enjoyed being out of the room for a little while. Michael and a few other people then walked me outside for a few minutes. The air was crisp but felt so refreshing. I had thought the day would never come when I could finally see the outside of the hospital again! The time outside ended way too quickly, but my body was wearing out and I needed to have the strength to transfer back into the bed. I had a very restful afternoon and that night enjoyed some fabulous Jim and Nick's BBQ with my officemate and her husband, who had come to visit. Overall, this had been a good day, and one I had been in desperate need of!

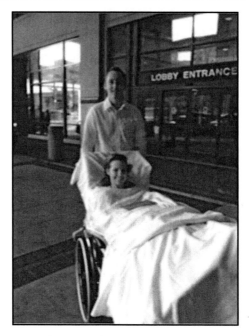

Enjoying a trip outside the hospital!

The talk of the past few days had centered on when I would be discharged and what the plans were after discharge. Because of how dependent I was on care, I did not at all feel like it was time to be discharged; however, infection risks were too high for me to stay at the hospital much longer. Had it not been for my parents' willingness to stay and take care of me, I would have ended up in a nursing home. I could not get up out of bed or even sit up in bed by myself. Thankfully, my parents both had amazing employers who allowed them to take the time off they needed to take care of me. My dad, the pastor of East Side Baptist Church in Thomasville, Georgia, had a great assistant pastor who gladly took care of things back in Georgia.

The school where my mom taught did what was necessary to make things work for the rest of the year. Then a friend of the family, Mr. Grubbs, who had been my fifth-grade teacher, volunteered to take Mom's place until she was able to come back. So many people willingly sacrificed to help us through that time.

Of course, financial concerns also plagued us. I had a wonderful officemate, Kari Showers, who took the time to set up a PayPal account and spread the word for people who wanted to help with the hospital bills. With the surgeries, medications, and hospital stay, the expenses were quickly escalating. So many people graciously donated and helped to cover some of these expenses. We also had a lawyer who offered to take and manage our case for us. His expertise over the next year would prove to be invaluable. God continued to pour out His provisions for us.

Also, my cousin Diana and her husband Alan stepped in to help. They had a beautiful home near Birmingham with a basement that would be perfect for my family and me. It was easy to enter and had a large sitting area, a guest room, and a full bathroom. We could easily put my hospital bed in the sitting room, where people could sit and visit. Then my parents would have a room of their own where they could get some rest. Diana and Alan graciously allowed us to invade their home for over a month! This was a blessing in more ways than one. It saved us a lot of money right at the beginning, it kept us close to Birmingham, and it gave me the opportunity to spend time with my cousin and her family.

While I was very thankful for a place to stay near Birmingham, I was very disappointed that I would not get to go back to Pensacola. Michael would have to start back to work and graduate school soon, and it would be hard to be away from him while he was in Pensacola.

Unfortunately, that was the only option we had. I would have to go to the doctors once a week for a while, and they wanted me there at first so they could monitor my therapy. It was going to be a challenge, but we were going to make it! Thankfully, the school where Michael worked, Pensacola Christian College, allowed him to rearrange his schedule so that he could have every Friday off to spend long weekends with me.

Things were falling into place and discharge was quickly approaching. I was nervous for the day to come but also looking forward to being out of the hospital. A few things still had to happen before I could leave, and one of those things included getting the stitches and staples out of my leg.

I awoke at 4:30 a.m. when one of the fellows walked into my room. He asked how I was doing, took a look at my ex-fix, and told me it was time for my stitches to come out. I looked at him and thought, "Are you serious?" Any hope of sleeping for the rest of the night was gone. I watched as he began the tedious process. My mom stood at my bedside counting as he took out each one of the stitches, and she lost count after 100. I started to feel bad for him because he looked so tired, and this was just the beginning of what I knew would probably be a long day for him. He talked with us as he carefully removed each suture. Apparently, he had come so early because he had to be at the OR by 6 a.m. However, he was still taking out stitches at 6 a.m. Finally, a little over an hour and a half later, he finished taking out the sutures and the staples. He quickly rushed off to the OR, and I attempted to get some more rest before the activities of the day.

On one of these last mornings in the hospital, I had just transferred into the chair when in walked the orthopedic surgeon who had fixed my left leg. Again, I am sure I had previously met him, but this was the first time I remembered meeting him. He and one of his fellows came in with their hands full. They had what looked like a tool set—which it actually was! He came over to me and got to business right away. He pulled up pictures and began to show me what exactly was on my leg and theoretically how they expected it to work. He explained to my family and me that we would have to adjust some of the equipment on the frame to hold appropriate amounts of tension to hold the bone fragments in place. Before he left the room that day, he told me that he needed to adjust the frame. He also warned me that it may be slightly uncomfortable. However, "uncomfortable" does not really adequately describe what I felt. I have no idea how to explain it. As he adjusted the frame, essentially placing pressure to adjust my bone, the sensation I felt reminded me of someone running their nails down a chalkboard, except, in my case, it was ten times worse and inside my leg. Frankly, it still makes me cringe when I think of how that felt. He also stressed that this might not work, but he was hopeful that as long as we did as we were instructed and kept up with the pin care, it would be successful.

Pin care...I hated pin care! Initially and for several months, we had to do pin care twice a day. It consisted of peeling off the Betadine-soaked gauze strips that had dried to my pin sites, as well as the leg hair that was around the site since I was not able to shave that leg. As each gauze strip was removed, it ripped off hair and scabs. Then, if that was not enough, Q-tips soaked in distilled water were used to scrub around each pin site. After this was done, each site was rewrapped with a strip of gauze soaked in Betadine. Each time we did pin care, it took at least an hour and sometimes longer, depending on how many people were helping. In fact, it was through pin care that I got to know Jennifer Geesling, who is now a close friend of mine. She came to visit while we were at the hospital and told my mom that she would come and help with anything we needed after we were discharged. Jen had graduated in my nursing class, but we had not hung out much in school. She lived in Birmingham, and when she heard about my accident, she decided to come visit. During the five months we were in Birmingham, our friend Jen came most of the nights and mornings to help my mom with pin care. She helped the process to go much quicker, saved me a lot of pain, and gave me company and support.

I was glad to have the frame adjustment over, but now on to discharge. Everybody was a little stressed about discharge. There were lots of things to work out to make the transition smooth. Issues with insurance had to be ironed out. Medical equipment and supplies— such as the hospital bed, a wheelchair, the hoyer lift, medications, and dressing change materials—needed to be purchased and set up. Also, we would have to notify the ambulance service to transport me from the hospital to my cousin's house. A lot of things still needed to be accomplished to make this discharge happen.

January 10: Discharge day! We worked all day trying to get everything organized. As the discharge time drew near, we realized that insurance would not cover the blood thinner I was taking. The hospital would not discharge me until I had that prescription filled. It was important to prevent me from getting blood clots. It was nearing 5 p.m. and I still had not been discharged. Thankfully, my Uncle Mark and Aunt Donna had come to visit that day, and they volunteered to go to the pharmacy for us and pick up my prescriptions and try to work out the issues. They were able to get the blood thinner and the rest of my prescriptions, and the hospital finally discharged me.

The EMTs arrived in my room to transfer me to the stretcher. That was what I had been nervous about all day—the transfer. I was worried that it would be extremely painful and that it would take days for me to get over it, but the transfer was not bad at all. We rolled out of the hospital and into the back of the ambulance and began the drive to our new home. I discovered on the drive to my cousin's house that someone needed to hold my ex-fix as we traveled. Because I had very little muscle control in my leg, my ex-fix rolled all over the place, and it was very painful, especially over the bumps. I discovered over the next few months that roads have a lot of bumps! Finally, we arrived at my cousin's home, and she and her family were outside to meet us. Her son was fascinated by the ambulance. He was so sweet and so concerned, and his smiles and giggles were an encouragement that helped get me through the next month.

CHAPTER 3

Basement Days

I had about one week to enjoy my new place before the doctor visits would begin. Actually, I can't say those days were "enjoyable." Each day was filled with taking medications, doing what therapy could be done, and trying to distract myself from the pain. My brother Tim and my sister both had to leave to go back to their jobs. This made me feel like my support system was falling apart! I had depended on them so much over the past few weeks for support and encouragement, and it was so hard to see them go!

Thankfully, we attempted the hoyer lift before my brother Tim left. The one we received was not as fancy as the one at the hospital, and there were no controls. It had to be manually pushed and maneuvered and the hookups were different.

There was a crowd for this first attempt. My husband, my parents, my brother, my cousin, and her husband were all there. They hooked up the sling to the lift and pumped me up into the air. They were struggling to figure out how to turn the lift as I dangled precariously in the air, but something was not right. I felt like I was slipping—probably because I was! By this point, I was dangling pretty high in the air over the hard floor. Luckily, my brother saw what was happening, caught me before I slid out, and then got me back to bed.

This incident was of course very painful. Needless to say, for the remainder of the time, I was always leery of the hoyer lift. Honestly, I think we all were.

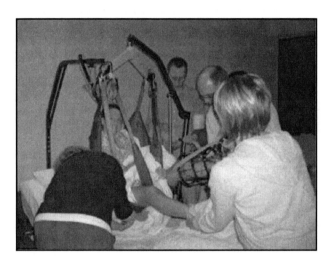

The hoyer lift

Over the next few days, I fought through hours of pain. Often, an hour before my pain meds were due, my joints and bones would begin throbbing unbearably, reminding me of how broken I was. I often sat and watched the clock, waiting for the next pain dose. I would wake up at night in pain, hoping it was time for another dose, only to see that it had been only an hour since the last dose. Many nights, I would quietly cry myself to sleep wondering when, if ever, the pain would stop.

Pain was not the only thing we had to deal with. My plastic surgeon had left in two drains in my lower abdomen where they had taken out my abdominal muscle. They were still draining too much to pull them out before we left the hospital, and he told us he would pull them during my next appointment. They were a big nuisance. Every time I attempted to sit up, the stitches holding the drain in place would pull on my skin and irritate it. Eventually, one of the stitches popped. I decided I was ready to be done with that drain. I asked mom to call my plastic surgeon to ask him if I could pull it. I was a nurse and had pulled out countless drains before, and I really wanted that drain out! As I have mentioned before, my plastic surgeon and I had a unique relationship. He told my mom to tell me that no, I could not pull out my drain and that I better behave! Although I was irritated that he would not let me pull the drain, his response did at least bring a smile to my face. It is common knowledge that nurses make the worst patients!

During this time, we realized that we needed more help. My cousin Dana volunteered to come from Costa Rica, where she and her family were serving as missionaries, to help with my recovery. Dana was a nurse, and I knew she would be a huge help! I was looking forward to seeing her, and I was glad to have someone who would push me to do what I needed to, even if it would be painful. I couldn't wait for her to get there after my appointments on Wednesday!

January 19: Every Wednesday was doctor day. I would see three of them that day. The day started early with the ambulance arriving at 6:30 a.m. The EMTs were great! They easily transferred me and were very careful not to jostle me too much. They joked with us and showed concern for what I was going through. They ended up having to spend pretty much the whole day with my family and me as they rolled me from place to place.

We started out in X-ray—oh, the dreaded X-ray! The cold, hard table they transferred me to was so uncomfortable. My ex-fix rolled around uninhibited, causing severe pain. The X-ray technicians were less than gentle as they attempted to move my joints in ways they just did not move. Unfortunately, it had to be done and the films had to be taken. Tears rolled down my cheeks as my legs and left arm throbbed with pain. The next pain pill dose could not come soon enough!

After X-ray, it was on to the plastic surgeon, who finally removed the drain in my lower abdomen that had been bothering me but chose to leave the other one in for another week. I also had another drain, a Penrose drain, imbedded in my flap. Originally, I had two of these Penrose drains, but one morning while I was still in the hospital, the plastic surgeon had come in to see me. While he was talking to me, he yanked out the drain without warning me. We all had a good laugh about it then, but this time I was ready for it. As he attempted to pull it out without my realizing it, I said, "I know what you're about to do." He smiled as he finished pulling the last Penrose drain out. He was very happy with how my flap looked and told me I could start hanging it down below heart level once or twice a day for a few minutes. This meant I could possibly start sitting up on the side of the bed, which would end up being a much harder task than it sounded! After seeing my plastic surgeon, I was in a much better mood and ready for my last two appointments.

We transferred over to another office to wait for the trauma doctor and the orthopedic doctor. Since I was on a stretcher, I was quickly taken back to a room, and we waited for the doctors to come. The reports from the doctors were overall fairly good. The elbow surgeon told us that I was laying down bone in my left arm and right leg, which was good, but it also meant that I needed to get moving to help the bone form and lay down correctly. The elbow surgeon and trauma doctor were both concerned that I had not started therapy yet, and they emphasized that it was a necessity and that time was of the essence. We had already been working on trying to get therapists to come to the house since I couldn't go anywhere without an ambulance transport. However, there had been a lot of problems with insurance. This would be the major concern and battle for the next week.

Finally, around 3 o'clock that afternoon, I got home. It had been a long day and I was exhausted. Soon, my cousin, her kids, and my aunt would be there. It would be good to see them, and I knew my mom would be really glad to see her sister. But right then, we all needed some rest after our busy day.

The week between my first two doctors' visits were a very frustrating time! Not only were there problems getting a therapist to come to the house for the therapy that the doctors had emphasized was extremely important, but I also had some serious bowel issues that caused me a tremendous amount of pain. Also, during that week, Michael had to return to Pensacola for his work and schooling, and that placed an added emotional stress on me. Since Michael had to leave, my dad spent hours on the phone trying to get someone to come help me with therapy. I did what I could on my own, with the help of my mom or Dana, but there were some things for which we needed the therapists. So far, no one would help. We were in desperate need of a wheelchair van so that I would not have to take the ambulance for transport. This was not a pressing need, but it would soon need to be met and weighed heavily on our minds. It seemed that as the week passed, the frustrations kept building with no resolutions.

January 25: It was appointment day again. This day would be a shorter day than the previous week, thankfully. I had to see only one doctor this trip. The EMTs arrived in the ambulance to pick me up. We had requested the same EMTs as the previous time, but unfortunately they were not able to come. This crew was far less understanding. As they picked me up for the transfer, my left leg got twisted. I cringed as sharp shooting pains went searing up my leg and a nearly unbearable ache set in. They quickly set me down on the stretcher, and my mom and Dana spent several minutes trying to situate my leg. I watched as the EMTs rolled their eyes and waited impatiently. I was to the point of tears by this point. We could not get my leg comfortable, and I felt the pressure of needing to just deal with it so we wouldn't waste more time. I knew, though, that if my leg was not secure, I would feel every single bump in the road to the doctor's office, especially since my leg was already hurting so badly. My cousin also had seen what happened and discreetly let them know how unprofessional they had been. Someone needed to stand up for me because I was definitely not in a condition to do so.

The doctor's visit was quick. I saw my plastic surgeon, and he finally pulled out the last drain from my abdomen. He said my flap still looked great and reminded me to start letting it down past my heart level some. Thankfully, after this visit we were done. We got back to the house and I crashed. My leg hurt so badly and the morning had exhausted me. I needed to just rest for the remainder of the day.

January 27: Finally, we were able to get a therapist to agree to come see me! My dad had spent countless frustrating hours on the phone trying to get things worked out, and finally he was successful! The company had agreed to give us six visits. It was better than nothing, and we hoped those six visits would be enough to get me to the next surgery. The therapist was supposed to call us the next day to let us know when he would be coming.

January 28: The therapist came to see me for the first time. This visit consisted mainly of an evaluation to see how rehab was progressing, which was not very far. He then spent some time working with my right leg. By this time, my right leg had stiffened and could barely bend at the knee. I gritted my teeth as he placed consistent pressure on it, trying to get it to bend. It moved some but not much. We unfortunately had a lot of painful work to do. I also had visitors from my home church in Thomasville that day! I loved having visitors! It helped me keep my focus off the pain and also helped wear me out some so I would sleep better at night. They were so encouraging and just what I needed at the time!

The next few days were fairly uneventful. While I needed the rest, those days seemed to be the hardest. All the extra time allowed me too much time to think. I often struggled with the frustration of all the constant pain, the twice-daily shots that I despised, the dreaded pin care, and of the unknowns of what would happen with my job, insurance, grad school, and the quality of my recovery—not to mention other minor nuisances, such as nausea and rashes that cropped up occasionally. Questions would flood through my mind. Would I ever walk again? Would I be able to one day be a nurse practitioner? Would I always have this unbearable pain? Would my leg ever heal? How long would recovery take? At this point, there was no light at the end of the tunnel. It felt impossible, and I struggled with not just physical brokenness but emotional and spiritual brokenness also. Each time during those struggles, I would eventually have to remember that it was not my responsibility to figure out the future — God already has that under control. It was my responsibility to focus on choosing to trust Him and His plan for my future. It is so easy to fall into focusing on the here and now when truly our focus should be on eternity. Any discomfort I feel for a brief time now may make all the difference for eternity.

February 1: It was appointment day again! That day, I was scheduled to see only the eye doctor. He wanted to check my vision once again and the orbital fracture status. On the previous day, I had pulled a significant chunk of glass out of my eyebrow area, and I wanted to see if he thought there was any more. I must admit that I was very nervous about this appointment. I have always disliked having anyone near my eyes, and I knew he would have to take a good look at my left eye. The nurse came in and put a numbing medication in my eye. That did not help my nerves at all, but they needed to check my eye pressure. It ended up being not too bad. The doctor then came in and did a few tests on my eye. He told me that I did still have a fracture and that I might still have a few pieces of glass work their way out, but he did not think we needed to do anything at that time. He tested my field of vision for any double vision, and there was only a little. He said that was remarkable considering the injury I had had, but if everything healed well, I would probably not need to do anything for my eye. For this, I was very thankful. The last thing I wanted was surgery on my eye!

The day ended up being a short one. Fortunately, we had great EMTs that day. In fact, one of them had at one time also had an ex-fix. It encouraged me to talk to him and see how well he had recovered. Again, the Lord knew what I needed, and as always, He had provided!

That morning had gone well, but that night we were presented with yet another problem.

I watched as Jen walked into the basement after a long day at work. I was glad to see her but knew what it meant: pin care time had come, probably my least favorite part of any day. When she walked in, she got a concerned look on her face. She walked over to where my leg was propped on pillows and took a close look at my big toe. My stomach began to churn. I had been concerned since we had been at the hospital that the boot that was putting pressure on my foot to prevent foot drop would cause a pressure sore. Several times previously I had had my mom move the boot around to redis-tribute the pressure, but with the amount of pressure being put on my foot, a pressure sore was inevitable. Now my fear was confirmed. Jen had stepped close to look at a black spot that had developed on my big toe. After close examination, we also noted one on my heel. Something would have to be done. We would need to call the doctors the next day to see what we needed to do.

First thing the next morning, we called the plastic surgeon. He had told us to call if we had any concern at all about infection. As soon as he found out what had happened, he emphatically told us to get rid of the boot because of a high risk that the sores would become infected. That was the last thing we would want to happen on that leg. And while I needed to quit wearing the boot, we also had to figure out a way to keep my foot up to prevent foot drop and to not hurt the flap. I did not have the strength in my leg to pull up my foot on my own. Developing this strength would have to be a priority over the next few weeks, but for now, we had to figure out how to keep that foot up.

It took all of us thinking together, including my therapist at the time, to come up with a contraption that would prevent any more pressure sores as well as keep all pressure off the already developed sores. We finally tried using a tongue blade glued to a thick strip of foam, covered with sheep's wool. We placed this on the center of my foot and then used the rubber tubing that had held the boot up and looped it around the back side of the tongue blade and tied it to my ex-fix to hold my foot up. We set an alarm to shift the placement of the contraption every two hours. Amazingly, it worked! And it was a lot more comfortable!

My appointment with my therapist that day was not as mild as my first evaluation appointment had been. He pushed very forcibly on my right leg, trying to get my knee to bend. I swallowed hard as I fought the urge to throw up from the nausea the pain caused. We had prayed so hard for this therapist to come, but right then I really wished he would go away. However, I knew it had to be done. Unfortunately, my joints were stubborn and they did not want to move. As he finished up with my leg, I knew I would be feeling that ache well into the next few days. But at least I had made some progress on my motion even if it was just a little. He moved to my arm next, and although it was also very painful, we had a little more success. I really liked my therapist, but after that day, I would dread each time he walked through the door.

The next day we received a visit from the pastor of the church that housed the school in Thomasville, Georgia, where my mom taught. Along with him, he brought cards, crafts, and snacks from the children and parents at the school. They were a tremendous support to me during my entire recovery. The cards made me smile, laugh, and cry. Knowing that so many people—even young kids—were praying for me to get better gave me the encouragement to keep pushing. We also found out that some friends of ours at Pensacola Christian College had "Praying for the McClures" bracelets made to give to those who donated to help us financially through this time. In addition, we saw God answer our prayers by providing a van for us to use once I recuperated enough that I did not need to be in a wheelchair. This was donated by a family from the school where my mom taught. What a tremendous blessing they were to us! All of these were powerful reminders that we weren't walking this journey alone. We had many brothers and sisters in Christ who were there cheering us on.

The next few days after that were rough ones. I got a stomach virus and was sick for two days. I also had a lot of pain in my left leg. At night, it would take me a long time to get comfortable. My mom would spend 15 to 20 minutes trying to stuff towels and washcloths under my knee and leg to stabilize the leg and help it not hurt so much. Because of the large rings on my leg and the need to keep it elevated, it was very difficult to get my entire leg supported. Often my knee would lack support and felt like it was overextending. We would stuff towels and washcloths under my knee until it was better supported. Many nights we could never make it comfortable, and those nights were usually long nights with little sleep.

Nights were always the most difficult. Everyone would go to bed, and I would be left to myself, except on the weekends when

Michael came. I did not have any distractions. It was quiet and dark, leaving me with only my thoughts and the pain. I remember being so frustrated as I struggled desperately to ignore the pain and go to sleep. My body needed the rest to heal and to be ready for the challenges of each new day. I would dread the nights, knowing that most would be a struggle. Thankfully, on Fridays and Saturdays Michael was there. Even though we often did not say much, just knowing he was there helped. He would pile up couch cushions and pillows in between my hospital bed and the wall so he could sleep close to me. We would lie there and hold hands as we both tried to sleep in the middle of the nightmare we were in. It was such a difficult time in our lives—but such sweet moments and memories were made as we walked through it together.

A new week had begun, and it started off with another therapy visit! I groaned when I saw the therapist walk in the door. I guess maybe I had hoped he would not show that day, but there he was. I had a bad feeling about that day, and I was about to find out why. He began working with my right leg, and as always, it caused extreme pain. I tried focusing on something else and breathing through it, but the longer he held it, the more it hurt. Eventually, nausea set in and then tears began to stream down my face, as I tried to cope with pain. All of a sudden, I started seeing black spots, and everything went blurry as my face paled. The therapist released some of the pressure and gave me a chance to recover a little before continuing to try to get my right leg to bend. I really disliked those visits, but I did appreciate that he was doing all he could to help me.

I had one day to recuperate, and then it was off to see the doctor again! As usual, I had concerns about the transport. I had begun to dread the trips back and forth to the doctor. The roads had countless bumps, and the ride was always very uncomfortable. This trip was no different, but nonetheless it was a necessary evil. At least I just had one doctor to see today—the plastic surgeon.

That day brought some great news! I did not have to keep my leg elevated anymore! I could actually sit up in a wheelchair without having to recline, and I could lie in bed with both legs—well one leg and one ex-fix—down on the bed. Hopefully, this would help the pain in my back and help me sleep better. The plastic surgeon also had his staff take out my stitches and clean off the blood and other fluids that had dried on my flap. My mom and Dana had attempted to do this before, but I had given them a hard time about it. First of all, it felt really weird when they pulled the pieces off, and I also was concerned that it might yank out one of the stitches. The stitches were gone now so I just had the weird sensation to deal with until they had the flap all clean. I have to admit, it looked much better once all of the dried-on drainage was removed. Overall, it had been a great day at the doctor's office, and I could not wait to see how my leg tolerated not being elevated.

Unfortunately, not having to elevate my leg did not make it any easier for me to sleep as I thought it would. My ex-fix rolled all over the place, twisting my knee uncomfortably, and I did not have the strength to keep it from doing so. We realized that we would still have to at least set it on one pillow to keep it from rolling. We also still needed to stuff towels under my knee and upper thigh because the ex-fix significantly elevated my leg off the bed and caused stress on my knee. That night was a rough one. The increased blood flow from not keeping my leg elevated made my leg somewhat uncomfortable, but eventually I got used to it.

The days in the basement were growing long. There were no windows, so I desperately missed the sun and the outdoors. I longed to be outside for just a few minutes. Each day I would look forward to the brief moments outside. It was winter in Birmingham and quite cold, but with all the blankets I had wrapped around me, I barely noticed the cold weather. The days that it was rainy or too cold were hard for me. On some days, there were not enough people to operate the lift to help me into the wheelchair until after 5 p.m., and I would miss getting to go outside. Those days were discouraging to me because it was the one thing I looked forward to each day. I would have to remind myself that at least I could get up and that I had people who cared about me enough to help me do so. My cousin, Diana, was the designated driver of the lift. She did such a great job and always made a point to be extra careful. My dad was the designated ex-fix holder. He was very careful to keep it perfectly still and not let it wobble everywhere. Mom, Dana, and Aunt Joanie alternated between holding my right leg up, guiding the actual sling, and directing everyone. Often, Diana's husband Alan would come down and help as well, especially if someone was unable to be there or busy running errands. It took a whole team to get the job done. We had many scares, and looking back on it now, it is quite humorous how nervous we were about it. But I still remember the knot in the bottom of my stomach that I would get each time I was suspended up in the air, dependent on only the seemingly flimsy sling to keep me from the severe pain of crashing into the floor. While I truly was thankful for all the help and for my cousin opening up her home, I also could not wait to no longer require the assistance of others. I longed daily to see the outside and to be able to transfer on my own into the wheelchair. Until that time came, though, each day I had to make the choice to be content and to patiently wait.

February 10: To my dismay, the therapist walked into the basement again. I actually did like him—just not what he put me through. I hoped that maybe that day it would be different. I really wanted to try to sit up on the side of the bed. Now that I could put my leg down, I thought it was time to try. When I told the therapist, he agreed that we could try it. We spent several minutes talking out the logistics and what to do with my left leg, and then finally it was time to attempt it. We set my bed up as far as possible to make it easier for me to sit up by myself. My cousin Dana helped adjust my upper body as the therapist helped with moving my ex-fix. My body actually swung around quickly, as each of us had an idea of how this would work. All of a sudden, for the first time I sat up on the side of my bed! It was amazing! A rush of emotions filled all of us in the room. We have several pictures of that moment. All of us had big smiles and were excited with how quick and easy it had been. In fact, it took me a minute to realize the odd sensation in my left leg. It had been two months since this leg had been dangled down, and my leg was letting me know it. It felt like it might explode, and at the same time, I felt extreme itchiness along with the sensation of many pins pricking me. It took quite a while for that sensation to go away. In the meantime, I took pictures with everyone and just enjoyed the moment.

Sitting up on the side of the bed for the
first time!

I still felt great; in fact, I felt so great that I thought I wanted to try standing on my right leg. We were halfway there so why not? Everyone else agreed, and with a deep breath and a lot of help from Dana and my therapist, up I went! The room erupted with cheers! A major step of improvement and a needed encouragement had just taken place. I had time for about one picture and a second to enjoy it before I became lightheaded. In just a few seconds, Dana and my therapist, helped me back into bed and put the head of my bed down. It was a reaction we all had expected and were prepared for. What an exciting day though! Not even the pain I was in after therapy could dampen my spirits that day.

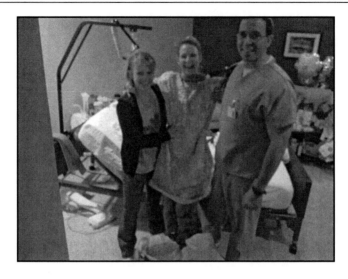

My first time standing up!

I spent the next day recovering from my therapy session and enjoying a visit from a family I had been close to all my life— the Williams family. The day was filled with laughter and conversation. As always, the visitors were good distractors and helped make some of the long days bearable.

The weekend had once again come, and my thoughts began to focus on what would happen the following week. The week would be busy. I would have therapy and several doctors' appointments in which many decisions would have to be made, and also I needed to figure out something for Valentine's Day for Michael. This week would be the first Valentine's Day for Michael and me as a married couple, and we would not even get to be together. The past couple of nights, I had cried myself to sleep about it. This was perhaps one of the more difficult emotional times I had to deal with. I had to constantly force myself not to dwell on how unfair things seemed and on how much Michael and I were missing out on during our first year of marriage. It was hard going through all of this with him rarely there, especially on days that should be special occasions. I could not even go buy him a card or get him anything for Valentine's Day. These thoughts plagued my already exhausted mind and emotions. I went through phases of anger and then discouragement until I finally came to the realization that in the big scheme of things, this one day really was not that big of a deal. Mom, Dana, and Aunt Joanie helped me to cope some. They bought card stock and stickers for me to use to make a card. Mom had to write in it because the nerve damage to my dominant left hand left me unable to write at the time. Jen also pitched in to help by volunteering to make a delicious chocolate cake for us to enjoy when Michael came that weekend. It made me feel better knowing that I could at least hand him something.

Several other thoughts raced through my head that weekend too. The following week we would learn when my next surgery would be. Bone grafts were going to be placed in my left arm and left leg where antibiotic spacers were currently residing. In my mind, once the surgery was completed, I should be able to go back to Pensacola to be with Michael. I also had concerns that the doctor taking care of my ex-fix would want to make major adjustments to the frame again. Now that my leg had a lot more sensation in it, I was really nervous about how painful it would be, especially after the previous time. For several weeks, I had been asking people to pray that this would not be the case. I had a sense of foreboding and dread as that week approached, and I was soon to find out why.

February 14: It was Valentine's Day and not only did I not get to see Michael, but I also had to have therapy. On top of that, I did not feel well and was fighting off exhaustion from the emotional battle I had been going through. This would be the sixth and last therapy visit. My therapist walked into the basement again and greeted us with a smile. In his hand, he held some colorful bands. He had brought me a Valentine's Day gift! I listened as he explained how the thera-bands worked and how much I would eventually use them. At the time, I was not familiar with them, but I soon would be. The rest of the therapy session included sitting up and standing for a few minutes again and then working on my range of motion on my right leg. When the session ended, I could see the therapist was a little sad to be leaving. He told us to stay in touch and to let him know if we needed anything. He had become a major part of my first step in recovery, and we were sad to see him go.

February 15: The dreaded day had come — doctor day. The ambulance arrived at 8:45, and the first stop was X-ray. As always, it caused some extreme discomfort. They did as much as they could while I remained on the stretcher but eventually had to place me on the cold, hard table to finish the films. Just the X-rays themselves exhausted me. Then it was on to see the doctors. The news was not what we had hoped. Though I seemed to be progressing well and my bones were healing, they did not feel it would be best to do my left arm and left leg surgeries together. They wanted to schedule my arm surgery and manipulation of my right knee for February 24 and my leg surgery for four weeks later. In the meantime, I would undergo intense therapy to get my elbow moving, as well as therapy to get my right leg strong and functional. As the news set in, my earlier sense of dread was confirmed. I would not be going home until at least April. It was yet another blow to my already discouraged heart. But the day was not over yet. Because my surgery would take place in a little over a week, I needed to go for pre-op. I was transported via the stretcher to pre-op, where we were placed in a very small, very warm little cubicle. By this time, it was 3 o'clock in the afternoon. I had not eaten anything all day because I was nervous about the appointment and then the discouraging news. As we waited and waited for the pre-op to be completed, I started feeling sicker and sicker. We waited for a couple of hours and still no one had come. The warmth in the room seemed to worsen, and all of a sudden my face became pale and I almost passed out. The EMTs with us ran and got some cool washcloths, and eventually I came back around. I made myself eat some crackers while we continued to wait. Not too long after that, the staff came to complete my pre-op, and we finally went home. By the time we arrived home, it was after 6 p.m., and after the exhausting, discouraging day, I just wanted to sleep.

The next day, Thursday, I had another discouragement because my cousin Dana had to leave. She had been such an encouragement and help to us the past several weeks! We were all sad to see her go, but she needed to get back to her husband and their ministry.

Later that day, Michael surprised me by showing up a little earlier than normal! It was great to see him and a huge encouragement at the time. I needed something to help me keep going, and his being there was a big help. We spent that night and Friday just hanging out and enjoying our time together.

Saturday came and once again we saw the Lord's provision for us. We had been praying and asking others to pray since we had left the hospital that we could find a wheelchair van for a good price. God had answered that prayer by providing us with the finances we needed to buy a van and helping us to find the perfect one. That day Michael and my dad went to pick up the van. I could not wait to go for a ride! I could barely contain my excitement! Finally, they came home and I got to roll my wheelchair, extended legs and all, into the van and go for a ride! This was the perfect ending to a very long week!

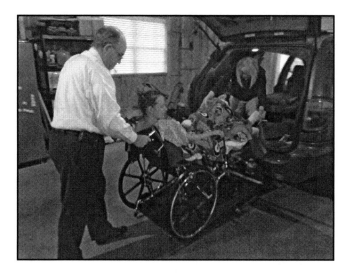

Getting to try out the new wheelchair van!

The next several days before surgery were spent trying to figure out what we would need to do since we would be in Birmingham for a much longer time than we had expected. We needed a bigger space for my therapy, and I needed to get out of the basement and be able to see the outside. Although the basement had been a perfect place at first, the four walls with no windows had become depressing, and

I needed to move somewhere else. We asked several people to pray for us in this decision, and dad began looking at different apartments. After several days, Dad told us that he had found an apartment that he thought would be perfect. We insisted that he take us to see it right away and it was perfect! There was a stream nearby that I could reach with my wheelchair. The apartment was spacious and had a huge window right beside where my bed would be and a spacious area full of trees right outside. It seemed perfect, and I could not wait to move there after surgery!

During that week, a group from my home church came to visit. Now that we had the wheelchair van, we were all able to go to a park and enjoy a picnic outside. It was a nice break from the normal routine. My dad also had to spend time trying to work out the details for the apartment. Our church offered to pay the rent for our apartment so that we could stay at a nice place! It was wonderful to see the Lord provide each step of the way as different needs came up.

Also, during this week before surgery, I had Skyped my brother Tim to see whether he and his family could come help us, since Dana had to leave. We were going to need the help. He wasn't sure if it would be possible but told me he would let me know. A few days later, he called back and said that they would be flying in the following Monday. I couldn't wait to see them! It gave me something exciting to look forward to and focus on as I faced my next surgery.

CHAPTER 4

Struggles In Moving Forward

*F*ebruary 24: Surgery day had come. The day started very early with the ambulance arriving around 4:30 a.m. We arrived at the hospital about 5:30 a.m. and were taken to a room so small that we could barely all fit. Mom helped me change into the hospital gown, and shortly after, the nurse walked in to draw blood and put in an IV. I watched her stick me several times trying to find a vein. By now, I was used to nurses not being able to find my veins. During my first stay, I remember once being stuck six times, and the nurses still could not find a vein. I pointed out to the nurse a vein that I knew would be the easiest to hit and finally she got it. We waited in the room for about an hour, and then someone came to take me back. My dad prayed with me and the others at my bedside, and I was rolled back to get the block in my arm. After they had parked my bed in a slot sectioned off by curtains, the anesthesiologist arrived and explained what to expect when he did the nerve block on my left arm. He said that he would be giving me some medication to help me stay calm, and it should also cause me to not remember them putting in the block. He also told me that he would be sending electrical stimulations down my arm that would make me violently twitch, to ensure they were in the right spot. I watched as they prepared to do the block, noticing the ridiculously long needle they would be using. I really hoped I would not remember anything.

As it turned out, I did end up remembering everything from the block, but it really was not too bad. Soon after the block was finished, they took me back to the OR. I faded out of consciousness as they rolled me into the operating room. During the surgery, doctors placed a central line in the left side of my neck, since getting IV access had proved to be very difficult. The central line gave them an easy access point to administer medications and draw blood without having to stick me every time. They also broke free some of the scar tissue in my right knee and bent it to full flexion. We were told that this took several tries. The residents tried first, and then finally the elbow surgeon came and got it to move. After they ranged my knee, they began the process of putting a bone graft into my elbow. They took the bone out of my left hip for the graft. The elbow surgeon also cleaned out my elbow, scraping off extra bone, and ranged my left elbow. Before sending me to post-op, they placed my right leg and my left elbow in a continuous passive motion machine (CPM). I had been instructed before the surgery to keep the CPM on all the time to keep the movement that had been freed up during surgery. I had been warned that this surgery would be a rough, painful one, and it was.

When I woke up in post-op, I struggled to catch my breath. Coughing hard a few times dislodged some mucous and made my breathing much easier. However, I noticed a nurse and one of the residents scurrying towards my bed. They anxiously asked me questions about my breathing and how I was feeling. They seemed nervous about something. I asked them what the concern was, and they informed me that my X-rays had shown a collapsed lobe in my right lung. They explained what could cause it and said that the most worrisome complication was a puncture from the insertion of my central line that might cause bleeding. The resident also mentioned that it could have been some mucous that plugged the lobe, causing it to collapse. At the time, I was not having any trouble breathing, and the last thing I wanted was to have them shove a chest tube in me while I was awake. I had seen and helped with that too many times as a nurse and had no interest in that happening to me. I told the resident to please knock me out if they had to put in the chest tube, but his response was not favorable. He said that they wanted a CT scan because they were concerned it was a vascular issue, and if that was the case, they would need to take me back to surgery. They quickly transported me to get the CT scan, which was complicated because of my surgery. Amazingly, through all of this, I remained relatively calm. I knew I was not having any issues breathing, and I really thought that the mucous I had coughed up initially had plugged the lung and caused it to collapse. Thankfully, that was the case. The CT scan showed significant improvement, and they finally were able to move me from post-op. They wanted to keep a close eye on me and my lungs, so they decided to put me in an ICU room for the night. Initially, that upset me, but by the end of the night I would be glad that decision had been made.

Once I arrived in the ICU room, I felt exhausted, and the pain in my right leg was starting to set in. At least the block in my left arm was keeping it numb for a while. My parents and Michael came in, but because of my exhaustion, I was not much company. Jen came for a visit later that night to check to make sure everything was all right. Eventually, everyone except Michael and my mom left for the evening, and between the seemingly endless respiratory treatments, I tried to get some sleep. As the night dragged on, my right leg began causing severe pain. We contacted the nurse, and she started icing the knee—20 minutes on and 20 minutes off. The cold helped to numb my knee some and made the pain bearable. The nurse was in our room several times each hour keeping the ice fresh and checking on how I was doing. She was a great nurse and very understanding. If we had been on a busy medical-surgical floor, I don't know how I would have made it through the night.

The X-ray technician showed up early in the morning for a chest X-ray. If I had been able to sleep, it might have annoyed me that it was so early, but since I had pretty much been up all night, it did not really matter. More painful bone X-rays came later in the morning, followed by the doctors. They had decided that I probably needed to rest instead of attempting therapy. It had been a rough surgery and an even worse night. I needed some time to recover. My chest X-rays had looked fine, so the doctor instructed me to just continue deep breathing and take my breathing treatments. They currently had me on oxygen through a nasal cannula, and I could not stand that thing in my nose! It dried out my nose, made it itch, and was just annoying. I kept trying to discreetly slip it off, but my mom and Jen did not miss much. Finally, I gave in and asked them to at least put some humidification on it.

I continued to get breathing treatments every few hours, and each time after them I felt awful. My heart would race, I felt like I would pass out, and it made me extra nauseous! I finally asked the nurses to discontinue the albuterol in the treatments, and they graciously agreed to do so.

That afternoon there were some problems with the CPM on my leg, so the therapist came to take a look at it and to do some teaching on it. The constant movement of my leg and the extra discomfort it caused were really wearing me out, but the day was not over yet. That evening, they decided to move me to a normal room on the orthopedic floor. Since I was already exhausted, the transfer ended up being a nightmare. My foot got slammed into an elevator door, and I was jostled around quite a bit. By the time we got to the new room, I was in tears. I just wanted a break—a break from the pain and a break from the constant interruptions to my sleep. Unfortunately, that would not be possible for a while.

Sunday the 26th started at 4 a.m. with lab draws, more breathing treatments, X-rays, and doctors—so much for getting some rest. My body was so exhausted that I could barely move! The labs came back and my blood counts were low, which partly explained why I felt so bad. In fact, the counts were so low I had to receive a unit of blood. Fortunately, after the unit finished infusing, I felt remarkably better. I still had nausea and pain, but the exhaustion was not as extreme. I hoped that by the next day, I would feel much stronger.

February 27: Therapy started again. Although the nausea was still there, overall I did feel a little better. The therapist came in the morning and worked with my right knee for a few minutes and then had me sit on the edge of the bed. I was able to bend my right knee over 90 degrees. That was huge! The excitement did not last long, however, as dizziness set in and I had to lie back down. When the elbow doctor came in to see me, she expressed her happiness with the movement of my left elbow and right knee. Now if only the exhaustion and pain would improve! However, all that movement had exacerbated the pain in my hip at the site where the bone had been removed, and now it compounded the pain from my left arm and right leg. For the remainder of the day I rested, knowing that because of the constant movements of the CPM and all of the blood draws, vitals, and breathing treatments I would have to have, I would not get much sleep that night.

A therapist showed up right on time the next morning. This time I was able to sit up on the side of the bed for a little longer before feeling nauseous and lightheaded. Another therapist came that afternoon to work with my right leg. She recommended that I use an electrical stimulation unit to help with the pain. Getting the necessary insurance approval was complicated, but eventually we got it. Again that night I ended up with little sleep as most of the night staff members were in and out of the room. The lack of sleep was beginning to wear on me.

February 29: I started that day thinking I would be discharged. I could not wait to get to the new apartment with my window view and to see my brother, his wife, and my niece and two nephews, who had arrived from Scotland. Most of all, though, I could not wait to have a night free of interruptions so that I could finally get some sleep. The lack of sleep was catching up with me. I just could not function on such little sleep much longer. The ambulance was on its way to pick me up, and the discharge papers were completed. Finally, I would get some rest! But, my hopes were about to come crashing down.

Apparently, there had been some miscommunication, and I could not be discharged. My doctor did not want me to go home until I could sit on the side of the bed and then transfer to the wheelchair with minimal assistance. I had attempted this before, but because of the nausea and dizziness, I had not been able to. My nurse, who had been great, came and relayed the bad news to us. Honestly, that was the last straw for me. As she walked out of the room, I was no longer able to conceal my emotional brokenness, and I began to just sob. I had not cried like that since before the wreck. The exhaustion, frustration, pain, and denied hope from the last two months all added to the sobs that now wracked my body. I could not hold back my emotions any longer. My mom and dad sat by the head of my bed and encouraged me to let it out. The anguished sobs continued and tears flooded down my face for over an hour. Finally, I composed myself just as my therapists walked into the room. They genuinely apologized for the bad news I had been given and asked whether I wanted to sit up and try to get in the wheelchair right then or wait until the next day. That was the wrong question to ask. I was frustrated and more than ready to get out of the hospital, and I would do whatever it took to get out. With determination, I sat up in bed, denied the questions they asked about dizziness and nausea, stood up on my right leg, and threw myself into the wheelchair. Everyone sat back in shock. Earlier that day, it seemed that it would be days before I could do this, but once again my stubborn determination had surfaced. Again, the therapist asked whether I was dizzy. Of course, I lied and said I was fine, when actually I was struggling to keep my eyes focused and swallowing back the urge to vomit. I wanted to go home, and nothing could stop me. I was unable to stay up long and required more help as I transferred back to bed, but I had done it. Now there was no reason for me not to be discharged—at least that is what I thought.

On the next day, once again I was able to transfer into the wheelchair, this time with much less dizziness and much more stability. I stayed up for a while as my brother Tim tried to figure out a way to stabilize my left leg and ex-fix, since my left knee still could not bend.

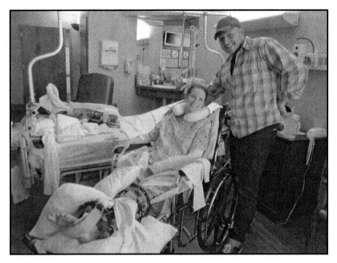

Ready to get out of the hospital now that my brother was
there to help!

After the smoother transfers, we got my discharge papers and finally headed out. We had been instructed that we must stop by to see the hand therapist for home exercises before we left the hospital. When we got there, there was some confusion. Apparently, my orthopedic doctor had not wanted me discharged until Friday, the next day, and my hand therapist did not have my therapy orders. She had to call my orthopedic doctor, who was not happy I had been discharged, to get the instructions. She did not have much time that day to squeeze me in because she had not been expecting me. Quickly, she reviewed my exercises with me and we scheduled my appointments for the next week. Then we rolled out of the hospital, strapped my wheelchair into the van, and off we went! Finally!

CHAPTER 5

Focusing On Recovery

I loved the new apartment! My hospital bed, with the leg and elbow CPMs attached to it, was in the living room and situated directly beside a double window overlooking a yard full of trees, birds, and squirrels. The living room was open, allowing me to see into the kitchen and dining room area, where everyone was during the day. My niece and nephews greeted me when I walked in the door. They brought a smile to my face, and their distraction helped me forget about the pain for a little while. Their enthusiasm and energy were contagious and brought smiles and laughter to all of us.

It was great, of course, to see Tim and his wife Amy too! Tim had been at the hospital the night before and that day to help me into the wheelchair. The therapist at the hospital had made sure that he knew how to use proper mechanics to help me transfer, but he did not really need much help. Until I could transfer on my own, Tim would be the one to help me get in and out of bed, encouraging me each time to need less and less help.

Amy was invaluable to us. She kept things clean, cooked meals for us, and helped my mom take care of me when needed. She also brought a tea from Scotland that helped me with my nausea; sometimes it seemed to be the only thing that would help the nausea go away. She also was great at back massages! My back would ache so much from having to constantly lie on it since the ex-fix would not let me turn at all. On the the nights that it was really bad, she would take time to rub out some of the sore muscles. What a blessing it was to have each of them there to help in their own special way!

The next few months were full of therapy, doctors' appointments, another surgery, and just day-to-day recovery. There were a few important happenings, but I will briefly summarize the rest of the time.

Intensive therapy started the Monday after I had been discharged from the hospital. In the meantime, I had been completing the home exercises my hand therapist had given me. I had to go to an hour of hand therapy and an hour of physical therapy three times a week. The first month or two, we did these both on the same day. Those were long days. Often, we would have to pack a lunch to eat quickly in between therapies, but sometimes we would wait in the lobby for a few hours in between. Our iPhones and iPads became our friends during those days as we all sat there and played games on them to pass the time away while we waited for my appointments. The therapy days were a family event. Tim used to tease me about having my entourage with me! He and both my parents would be there, as well as Michael when he was in town. I am sure we got more than a few weird looks with the contraption on my wheelchair supporting my left leg and the entourage surrounding me, but what an amazing thing to have such a wonderful, supportive family. I couldn't have done it without them.

On the first day of therapy, I was nervous. First, I went to hand therapy, and the therapist spent the first few minutes trying to figure out how to best work with me, since I was in a wheelchair with my leg sticking out and they needed me to be sitting at a table. After figuring out how to work around that, the therapist started to work on bending my arm. This proved to be a difficult and discouraging task, and the progress was slow, painful, and often unrewarding, despite our best efforts at therapy and at home.

Working hard at hand therapy!

After hand therapy, it was off to physical therapy. That day was just an evaluation day. They needed to see how far along I was and where they should focus their energies. Since I could barely transfer from my wheelchair, I had a long way to go. Actually, I should have been in a home therapy program, but my orthopedic doctor had been insistent that I go to the outpatient therapy gym. I imagine I was one of the most injured patients they had ever seen. The therapist I saw was sweet and understanding and I liked her a lot. She told me at the end of the day that she would work with me some but thought it would be best if I saw another therapist who had experience with trauma cases like mine. I would schedule my next few appointments with her. In the meantime, I was given more home exercises to do. As if I didn't have enough to do already.

Because of the ex-fix, I could not even wear normal clothes. It had proved impossible to get anything over the large rings. Thankfully, a friend of ours had made me several pretty gowns, and we had also received a gift from another friend from a company named Annie & Isabel. They made adorable hospital gowns, and I had received a couple of those. The company also asked whether they could post my story on their site so that other people could know about me and encourage me in my journey. It really was encouraging when other people reached out to help.

On days I did not go to therapy, I still did therapy at home. We set alarms on our computers to correspond with our other electronics. They had different beeps for each time medications were due or when it was time to do another round of therapy. It seemed like all day there was a never-ending chorus of alarms going off. My brother Tim was responsible for helping me do my therapy exercises. I think our favorite was the skateboard. I would set my right foot firmly on the skateboard, and he would push it back until it could not go any further. He would hold it there for a little while and then gradually continue pushing it back, reminding me every once in a while that I still needed to breathe! I would squint my eyes and grit my teeth through the whole thing since it felt like the muscles in my legs were on fire. But I continued to keep a smile on my face and laugh and joke about how much it hurt! Each time we worked, significant progress was made. Gradually, I was getting more and more range on my right knee. The least favorite of the therapies was the elbow. I cannot even begin to explain how painful bending that elbow was. I would lie in bed and Tim would place a consistent pressure on my elbow to get it to bend. We would work on this for about 15 to 20 minutes each session. I know it was hard for him to see me hurt like that. I went from joking around to ignore the pain to solemnly trying to hold back tears, unsuccessfully on some occasions. I sincerely hoped that one day that pain would pay off.

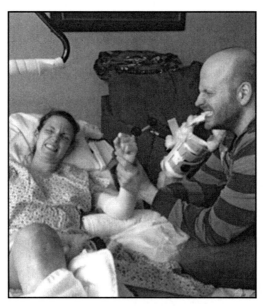

Tim helping me with bending my elbow while
doing therapy at home

On one of my particularly tough days when I struggled with the immense pain I was in, my mom came over to my bedside to talk with me. As she sat there close to tears, she asked me if I ever wished I had just died in the accident. It was a difficult question to answer, because I did not want to be untruthful. Truthfully, there had been many times that, because of the intense pain I daily experienced, I wished that I had not made it through the accident. I often wondered whether I would ever get back any quality of life because of all the pain that I continued to experience. I did not want to upset her by telling her about those times, but I chose to be truthful. I told her at times I had wished that I had not made it through the accident. I watched the pain in her eyes as she told me that she had wondered whether she should not have prayed so hard that God would save my life and wondered if they should not have made the life-saving choices for me that they made. It was difficult to see my mom carrying such a heavy emotional burden. I realized that while I had hard physical and emotional battles to fight, I was not the only one struggling with emotional brokenness. This was a fight my whole family in their own specific ways had to struggle with as we daily trudged through this trial.

Some of our days would drag on—especially the days that I did not have therapy. There were more than a few days that I fought against severe discouragement as I became overwhelmed with my physical brokenness. Progress was slow and it seemed like the end was nowhere in sight. I knew I had made progress, but I thought I should have been much further along. I was hard on myself and some days lost the battle with discouragement. I would lie quietly in my bed, not really saying much but passively doing my exercises and barely eating anything as I allowed myself to become consumed with emotional brokenness. I focused on how much pain I was in and was discouraged that it felt like it would never get better. I focused on the things I could not do and on how much I missed Michael. Thankfully, the Lord gave strength. When my determination surfaced again, I threw everything I had into getting better.

The work to get strong enough to get up and stay up started the next day at therapy. I met my therapist, Kim Ingram, who would work with me for the remainder of my time in Birmingham. She was great and just what I needed. She was empathetic to my situation but not afraid whatsoever to show some tough love at times. With the help of my therapist and the parallel bars at therapy, I started trying to stand on my right leg for longer periods of time. I still could not put weight through my left leg because of the antibiotic spacer where the bone graft needed to go, so I was able to use only my right leg to stand. Each day, we set a goal for how long I needed to stay standing. Kim would give me a time frame, and I would stay standing for that period of time. She would tell me I had to do it twice and then after the second time made me do it again. She was sneaky but knew how to push me to get as far as I could. It was discouraging at first because I could barely stay standing for a minute, but amazingly, the next time the minute was no big deal. Thankfully, I began quickly progressing. Unfortunately, my elbow therapy was not going as well. My elbow continued to get stiffer without gaining much more range even though we worked it constantly and I remained in my CPM while I was in my bed. There was still much work to be done on it.

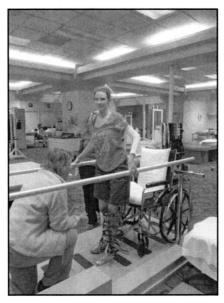

Working on standing on just
my right leg

Finding a way for me to wear normal clothes also made it to the top of our priority list. Through the creative juices of everyone but me (somehow I missed out on the creative gene), we figured out a way for me to wear a pair of shorts for therapy and out around town. My mom and Amy bought several pairs of shorts, cut them up the side seam, and inserted a zipper. Once I had pulled my shorts over the ex-fix, I could zip the side seam up. This worked perfectly! It was nice to finally be in normal clothes once again.

On March 15, we achieved another milestone: I went out to eat for the first time since the accident! My brother's birthday was the next day, and since I would have a doctor's appointment as well as therapy, which would be exhausting, we decided to celebrate a day early. It was another first and a nice change from eating at home in the bed or occasionally in the wheelchair.

The next day, March 16th, I had my appointment with the orthopedic doctor responsible for my left leg. He requested a few X-rays for the next procedure they needed to do. While doing my X-rays, the technician asked me to move my left leg. Because of the very heavy, metal ex-fix as well as atrophied muscles, I told him I could not lift it. Very bluntly and impatiently, the technician told me that it was really bad that I could not lift and move my leg. Perhaps if he had been a little kinder about it, I would not have been as upset, but the way he spoke had been unkind and without consideration to what I was going through. It really did upset me, and it worried me that I was not doing what I needed to be doing to get better. Thankfully, I had my appointment right after so I could check with my doctor about it.

The X-rays showed that my left leg was not healing as well and as quickly as my other fractures. However, during the next surgery, they would be able to remove a few pins and adjust the frame again. They also needed to remove the antibiotic spacer above my knee and replace it with a bone graft, but first they needed to check for infections. If there was no infection, they could proceed with the graft, but if there was an infection, they would replace the antibiotic spacer with another one and wait six more weeks before trying the procedure again. As long as the antibiotic spacer was in, I could not put weight on that leg, which meant I could not begin learning to walk again. Putting weight on the leg was also necessary to help the fractures in my lower leg to heal. My doctor also explained that they would need to remove some hardware from my kneecap since it had healed, clean up the scar tissue and extra bone, and range my knee to help me get more motion in it. We all hoped and prayed there would be no infection so progress could continue, but we would not know until surgery day.

During the appointment, I told my doctor what had happened in X-ray. He agreed that it probably could have been handled better but that what the technician had said was true. He wanted me to work on lifting and controlling that leg, and it did really concern him that I could not lift it. Now I really was determined to lift that leg!

I had therapy that day, and that is what we mainly focused on. I could barely lift my leg an inch off the therapy table, and it took every ounce of energy to do that; however, with hard work and determination, two days later, I lifted my leg all the way up in the air. The first time I did it, I surprised myself! Once I got it up a few inches, it was much easier. Those first few inches were tough though. We were all so excited that we even made and posted a silly video online of my brother pretending to use his mind to lift my leg. It allowed everyone who had been praying for me and keeping up with what was going on to see us having fun with my progress. I guess that laughing and being ridiculous is sometimes necessary to make it through tough times. It did make for some pretty funny memories!

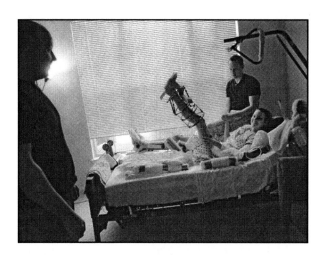

Finally able to lift my leg in the air!

The four weeks until my next surgery went by relatively quickly. This period was filled with a lot of pain, but there was also a lot of encouragement. Several of my friends from Pensacola Christian College, where I had worked, came to visit, as well as some old friends from my home church. They were all very encouraging. Every day, I had received cards, gifts, and financial support from others. I looked forward to the arrival of the mail each day because it always brought a smile to my face. It was a daily reminder of how many people were cheering me on. I had the opportunity to watch the Lord provide daily for our every need through the support of His people. We had many expenses! I did not have a job, my parents were not working, and Michael was in graduate school and not bringing in much, yet we had enormous hospital bills and needed to buy medications and medical supplies, food for all of us, and gas for transportation to and from therapy and appointments. God's people proved so faithful and loving! Through their support, each one of our needs was met.

March 22: Surgery day again! I felt nervous going into the operating room, wondering if I would be infection-free and could finally have the bone graft done. I dreaded the pain that I knew would follow the ranging of my left leg and possibly my right leg also. As I drifted off to sleep, I found comfort in knowing that this should be the last major surgery for a few months.

When I woke up, I immediately asked how the surgery had gone and whether the bone graft had been done. The resident was there, and he smiled and said that I had been infection-free and that the bone graft had been completed. However, it was not all good news. When they attempted to range my left knee, my kneecap had cracked. We would have to take extra precautions when moving it to make sure it healed correctly. The fractured kneecap did not even faze me. I was so excited that the bone graft had been done so I could start to really make some progress.

Once I returned to my hospital room after surgery, I visited with my family, including my sister Charity, who had come from Hawaii to visit during her spring break. Then I got some much-needed rest. Therapy would start the next day and I would need to be ready.

The next day, therapy started bright and early. Usually, I would wake up extremely nauseated in the mornings until I ate something and gave myself some time to wake up. The therapists came in right as I was waking up, and I told them I could not get up yet because I knew I would throw up. This was partly true, but I was really just too grumpy and lazy feeling to get up and put myself through pain. Thankfully, they were gracious enough to give me an hour to pull myself together. It was a smart decision because had they not, we all would have been miserable. When they came back an hour later, I was ready to go. They showed me the precautions to take when working with my left knee and then had me get up with the walker. It took a few minutes to get everything organized because I had drains, an indwelling pain pump, and IVs attached to me that all had to transfer with me. Once we got everything set, I sat up, oriented myself for a few seconds, and then, with the help of my therapist, pulled myself up to the walker. It was hard to balance on just my right leg so I could not stay up long, but I took a couple of hops forward on my right leg with the walker and then backwards back to the bed. With my fractured kneecap and the new bone graft, it would be a few more days before I could put weight on that left leg, but at least I could hop a few steps with the walker. That was progress! A couple of my friends who were there for a weekend visit cheered as they celebrated with me another step forward!

This hospital stay was not nearly as long as the previous one. On Day 4 after my surgery, I was discharged. The few days in the hospital had gone as well as could be expected. Most days consisted of two therapy visits and then resting to recover from the therapy. By the end of the stay, I had been able to put a little weight on my left leg, and things seemed to be going pretty well. Unfortunately, that was about to change. Before I left the hospital on the last day, the therapist had really worked hard on my left leg, causing a lot of pain. My pain had become somewhat out of control when I came off the patient-controlled pain pump the day before, which increased the pain caused by therapy. Sometimes when the pain got out of control, it would be days before we could get it controlled again, and this was one of those times. The pain had become nearly unbearable by the time we got back to the apartment. When I transferred from the wheelchair to the bed, I barely made it, which scared everyone who was there with me. The transfer, for some reason, caused more pain then normal, and I grimaced as my legs throbbed. Then the tears began to fall as the fatigue, frustration, and pain of the day overwhelmed me. But the rough day had not ended yet. As the pain edged off slightly and I lay motionless in bed, nausea set in. I spent the rest of that night and the next day throwing up everything I put in, including pain medication. Finally, the next evening, I was able to keep some food down, and I started feeling better. That was good, because the next day we were about to embark on two months of intensive therapy.

March 30: We hit the ground running on my first day of therapy. I finally could put some weight on my left leg, which meant I could start the long process of learning how to walk. At this time, I did not realize how long the process would be, but I did realize that for the next few months, I would have to face my life one day at a time, one step at a time. Looking at the big picture of what had to be done was too overwhelming and discouraging. My focus had to remain simple, making the most of each day. I had to set attainable goals and give everything I had to reach them. The Lord had set before me a large task to accomplish, and I constantly had to remind myself that with His strength it would be accomplished.

The first step was accomplished on that first day of therapy! That day, I got up and walked with a walker for the very first time! My dad stood by my side ready to catch me if my legs gave out as I took each step forward, and Tim and Michael stood at the "finish line" encouraging me on with each step I took. Exhausted, I finally reached the "finish line" and collapsed on the table. Of course, I had relied heavily on the walker for support, but I had done it. For the first time since the wreck, I had taken steps. Tears filled the eyes of all those around me. This accomplishment came months before the doctors had originally thought it would be possible and had been the result of a lot of hard work and pain. I was not done yet though, and my therapist was merciless! She looked at me and said, "All right, let's do it again." I looked at her like she was crazy but saw there would be no changing her mind, so up I went. By the end of the day, I had reached the "finish line" four times! These were amazing steps forward and a much-needed encouragement. Sadly, my mom was not there. She had the same stomach virus I had had and had to stay home. But thank God for technology! My brother recorded it so she and all our prayer partners on Facebook could share in that moment. That evening, we watched as our Facebook pages "blew up" with comments and "likes" as people around the world celebrated with us the first steps on my road to recovery.

Walking for the first time since the accident!

The months of April and May were once again focused on therapy and recovering. I went to therapy every weekday and continued to do more exercises at home. We focused on building my strength so I could walk better and on gaining range of motion in my knees and left elbow. My right knee made great progress during this time, but my left knee and elbow continued to cause problems.

Right before my left leg bone graft in March, I had seen Dr. Stewart, my elbow doctor, and she had not been happy with the progress in my range of motion. She had scolded me, telling me I needed to work harder on the range of motion. It had been a discouraging day. I had been working so hard to get it to bend, ending up in tears most days because of the pain. However, she knew there was just a short window to get it moving, and she wanted me to understand the seriousness of it. I did understand it, and even though the report had been discouraging, I took her advice and worked harder on it. She ordered a splint for my elbow to be used for 20 minutes several times a day. Whenever the splint was on, I would tighten it every 5 minutes, forcing my arm further into either flexion or extension, depending on which one I was working on that day. Unfortunately, even with the splint and hard work at therapy, my elbow seemed locked and barely gained any range.

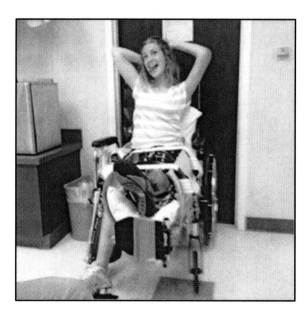

Trying to have some fun during elbow therapy!

My elbow may not have been gaining range, but I did continue to gain strength in my forearm and left hand. Because of damage to my ulnar nerve during the wreck and the following surgeries, I had no sensation in the pinky side of my hand, which extended down into that side of my arm. The nerve damage greatly affected my ability to use my hand. We were told that some improvement was expected as the nerve tried to heal but that it would never be normal and that I would not recover full functionality. Initially, I had hardly any grip strength and very poor dexterity. That prevented me from spreading my fingers apart and from bringing them together. One of the hardest things I had to cope with was knowing that I could never play the piano with ease as I had in the past and would never be able to play the guitar again. These had been stress relievers and a way to unwind but would now just be a painful reminder of what I lost during the accident. Also, on top of everything else, I had to learn to use my right hand as my dominant hand. I could not pick up and hold a fork, much less attempt to get food on it and then try to somehow bend my arm far enough to get it to my mouth. Fortunately, I had quickly adjusted to using my right hand for everyday tasks but had not been successful with writing with it. About the middle of April, although very shaky, I began to have the ability to write again. Being able to write gave me a way to cope with all the emotions I had, and I began to journal some of my thoughts. A few of these excerpts will be included throughout the rest of this book, as they express some of the raw emotions I felt at certain phases of my recovery.

While most of this time consisted of day-long therapy, there were a few days of excitement, as well as a few discouraging days.

April 8: Easter Sunday. I had not yet been able to go to church since the accident. On most Sundays, I had needed the day to recover from therapy and prepare for the strenuous week ahead, but now, finally, I had the strength to start going to church. My dad has been a pastor all of my life, and my church was an extension of my family. It constituted a significant portion of my life. My home church consisted of people who were like family to me, and I wanted my first time back at church to be spent and shared with them. We decided that it would be fun to surprise everyone by walking with my walker into church that morning. It would be the first time many of them had seen me walk. No one knew we were coming, and though the journey home was rough, long, and uncomfortable, it was well worth it.

I greatly underestimated the emotion of that moment. When I walked into the auditorium, I saw the surprised faces of those who cared so much for me turn from unbelief to unhindered emotion as they rose to their feet and applauded while I finished what seemed an unending walk to the pew. They cheered—not for me but for what, in that moment, I represented. They saw a sinner who had undeservedly received the outpouring of grace from an awesome God—a sinner who like them could call on an all-powerful God for strength and healing because of what He had done on the cross for me. Had it not been for His sacrifice in giving His life to pay the penalty for my sin, had it not been for His grace in extending that gift to me, and had it not been for His love in welcoming me into His family when I reached out for His gift of saving grace, I would not be where I was that day. We celebrated what made it all possible: His death and resurrection. As long as I live, I will never forget that special day.

My family and I at church on Easter!

We also reached two other big milestones during that weekend trip! For the first time since the wreck, I slept in a normal bed with my husband instead of my uncomfortable hospital bed. We were nervous about how it would go, since Michael tends to move a lot when he sleeps, but I think that he was so concerned about hurting me that he didn't budge all night. Words cannot explain how comforting it was to finally be able to sleep next to him again. From that night on, I never slept in my hospital bed. Also, during that weekend, I got to take my first shower since the wreck. Up until that point, I was only able to do sponge baths, but since I finally had the strength, we had figured out a way to get me in the shower without messing up the dressings around the pins on my ex-fix. It was amazing! I never wanted it to end! No more sponge baths! What a great weekend! Things really were starting to progress!

Around that same time, I had another doctor's appointment for my leg. The news was not encouraging. The doctor said that the leg still was not healing well, and it would most likely be at least 3 to 4 months before the ex-fix could come off. I had begun to grow very tired of the large ex-fix on my leg. I grew concerned that my leg would never heal. I asked my prayer warriors for prayer regarding its healing. I requested others to pray that for my birthday, on May 24, we would get news that my leg had healed and the ex-fix could come off. It became known as the May 24th miracle, and I knew many people were praying and truly believed it would happen. I had over a month until then, plenty of time, in my mind, for our miracle. In the meantime, I stayed busy.

Although therapy really did occupy most of my time, I also got to enjoy some time with my niece and nephews. I enjoyed mornings with my niece Cara. She loved to watch me put on makeup and loved to pull off the silicone strips we placed on all my scars at night. She thought they were "band-aids." They did somewhat resemble band-aids but fortunately did not stick as bad. We would pull them off and place them back on the plastic they came from and look to see whether they had helped my scars. They seemed to make a difference at least on the scars on my face. Her smiles and giggles helped to put me in a good mood each morning, giving me a great start to each day. I also enjoyed several trips to Toys "R" Us, watching Garrett and Cara run around excitedly to see all the toys. We celebrated Brendan's first birthday and went to the park or McDonald's play place. Most of all, I just enjoyed spending time with them at the apartment. Many days, they brought just the encouragement that I needed.

At Toys "R" Us with my niece
and nephew!

Each morning as we prepared to go to therapy, it would take almost an hour for us to get my ex-fix strapped onto the one skinny leg attached to the wheelchair. I still could barely bend my knee, so the leg of the wheelchair had to be adjusted to protrude straight out from the wheelchair. We then had to balance the ex-fix on top of the skinny leg of the wheelchair and somehow get it strapped down so it wouldn't roll. It required several pillows and gait belts, which never really held the ex-fix well. Finally, Tim came up with an ingenious invention to hold my ex-fix. He attached a board to the leg of the wheelchair and then nailed half of a large cylinder of cardboard to that wood board, after, of course, spray-painting it pink. We placed a pillow in the bottom of the half cylinder, and my ex-fix rested perfectly in it. This saved so much time and was much more comfortable than what we had been using. We would really miss Tim, Amy, and the kids when they had to leave, which would be soon.

April 24: Tim's family had to leave to go back to Scotland, and I spent the last few minutes of that morning with Tim at Starbucks. I wished he could stay longer, but I was so thankful for the time that he and his family had been there and for all they had helped us get through. They would really be missed, but I still had a lot of work to do and needed to focus on getting better.

My Journal Entries:

First Entry 4/29/12: God loves me more than anyone else ever could. Anything allowed in my life is because He loves me. No good thing will God withhold from those who love Him. My current state is what is good. With an eternal focus, I can see that handled with the right heart, my trial will be what is best for me. If not rewarded in this life, it will be in eternity.

His presence…not always felt but always present. Many times there is frustration in my spirit because I cannot feel Him. If only my heart could firmly rest in His promise to always be there.

Humility…dependence upon others…upon God for absolutely everything, including my future disforming scars and crippled joints that will last a lifetime. A constant reminder to remain humbly under God's control.

4/30/12: Loneliness is often a struggle. I am surrounded by people who dearly love me but still I feel lonely. I feel as though no one understands fully what I am going through. I can't really explain the emotions that I experience to anyone and that is so hard. It's hard to go through the pain and emotions alone.

It can be hard not to get frustrated with people who say it's going to be okay. I know in their hearts, their intentions are pure and they just want to encourage, but I struggle to not say that it's easy for them to say because they are not facing being crippled the rest of their life. However, I know that is just coming from a fleshly heart that is struggling to accept what God has allowed in my life. I struggle because I turn my thoughts to myself and selfishly focus on what I want. I am learning that this temporary life should not be my focus but rather the influence I can have on eternity! One day, God will fully heal my body and there will be no more pain, suffering, and embarrassment, but when that day comes, what will I have to show for this trial? Will God be pleased with what I made of this trial? Will my focus be turned from myself and how my fleshly mind views this situation, or will I learn to rely on God to give me strength to view this through His eyes and the difference I can make for Him throughout all eternity. I think the most important thing I have learned is the importance of living life with my focus on eternal not temporal things.

May 3: My next doctor's appointment. We didn't get the news that it was time to get my ex-fix off, but we did get some good news. My leg was healing! The bones at the top of my lower leg were healing well, but the ones on the bottom were taking a little longer. The doctor said that by the next month, the ex-fix should be ready to come off. That was very encouraging! I also got permission to be full weight-bearing on my left leg. This, of course, made my therapist happy, and she rapidly amped up the intensity of my therapy sessions, including more walking with just a cane instead of a walker and building up strength to climb stairs. Progress was happening, just not as quickly as I wanted it to.

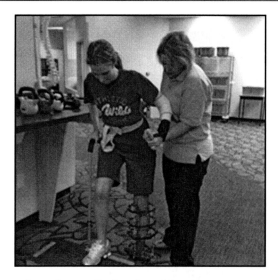

Learning to climb stairs with using my cane

My Journal Entries:

5/4/12: If given the choice by God to stay on earth or go into eternity with Him at this current moment, selfishly, in my mind, I would choose the latter, but in my heart and in my desire to serve the Lord, I know that would be selfish. God left me here not because I deserve to be here or even because He knew I wanted to be here but because in His all-sovereign plan, He still had a purpose for me to fulfill—a sobering and at times scary thought. How privileged I am to be valued enough by God that He chose to use me and left me here on this earth to accomplish that purpose. What a weight I now carry on my shoulders to not disappoint Him.

Next on my agenda was moving back to Pensacola. I was so ready to be home, and now that doctors' appointments would be once every six weeks, it might be possible to return to Pensacola soon, provided

I could get into a good therapy gym. We began to make preparations for the move, with the temporary move date set for June 2.

We stayed very busy the month of May. Now that I could travel a little more easily, we were free to make a few trips. One of those trips was to Pensacola to see the nursing students I had taught the year before get pinned. My nursing students meant so much to me and had been a huge encouragement to me through everything connected with the accident. I wanted to be there with them in that important moment in their lives. We did not know for sure that things would work out for me to go, so we did not tell many people. In fact, just a few days before we were to leave for the ceremony, I had another awful experience.

May 4: It had been a good day at therapy, but now something just did not feel right. I did not feel well, and my back really was bothering me. I hoped that resting would help it some, but unfortunately, that was not the case. At 1:30 a.m. I jolted awake. The pain in my back was now unbearable! It hurt so much I could barely breathe. The nausea was overwhelming, and I knew it would be only a matter of minutes before I vomited. I sat up, trying to find some position that would relieve the pain, but nothing helped. I woke Michael up and had him wake up my mom. I needed to go to the ER because, by this point, I knew that I had a kidney stone and that I needed something to help with the pain. Minutes later, I began violently vomiting the most disgusting, acidic vomit ever, worsening the pain. We quickly loaded up and got to the ER. Thankfully, they weren't busy, and they got me right in and got some medication in me. They took me to have a CT scan done, and once I returned to my cubicle, I drifted off to sleep from the effects of the pain and nausea medication. Meanwhile, my parents and Michael sat in uncomfortable chairs, not sleeping, while we awaited the results. As expected, I had a kidney stone and would just have to wait until it passed. The next few days I continued to have pain from the stone and still didn't pass it. We thought I would not make it to the Pinning Ceremony, since it was just a few days away, but thankfully, a day before we were to leave, I finally passed the stone.

May 9: Pinning Ceremony Day! Very few people knew I would be there. I had told only a couple of my friends on the faculty who would need to help me and had also coordinated things with the chair of the department. She told me that they would love to have me sit on the platform with the other instructors for the ceremony. It meant so much to me that they allowed me to do that! Now I could see the face of each of my students as they came on the platform to be pinned. My friend Lindsey met us outside the auditorium and helped wheel me back to where the faculty were waiting to go on stage. The look of surprise on many of their faces was priceless! It was so good to see all of my coworkers again. They had all prayed so much for me and done so much to support me. I enjoyed a few minutes with them backstage, and then we lined up to go on the platform. Lindsey and I were last in line. As she rolled me onto the stage, I could hear the whispers of people as they started to figure out what was going on. Then I saw smiles on the faces of many of my students as they saw me. Again, words cannot describe this moment for me. I was thrilled to be able to be a part of this special time in their lives! After the ceremony, I got to talk to and take pictures with many of my students, creating more special memories during my journey.

Enjoying getting to see my coworkers at the
Pinning Ceremony!

My time at home in Pensacola did not last long, and it was time
to go back to Birmingham on Sunday. Now I really could not wait
to get home permanently. In just a few more weeks, I would be back
home with Michael for good, but we still had a few details to work
out before we could go, including getting good therapists. While we
had been in Pensacola for the Pinning Ceremony, we visited several therapy gyms, trying to find the right place. We left most of the
places feeling discouraged and concerned. Finding the right place for
therapy would be crucial for my recovery. We knew my therapy and
the skill of the therapist would play a significant part in the quality
of my life following my recovery from the accident. We asked many
people to pray for doors to open and for us to find the right place
for therapy. The only gym that we had felt positive about was the
rehabilitation center at Andrews Institute for Orthopedics & Sports
Medicine. They had both physical therapy and hand therapy there in
the gym, and it had been recommended by my doctors and therapist
in Birmingham. However, I would have to get approval to go there,

and I would have to "jump through hoops" with the insurance company. Over the next few weeks, we worked to get settled and finally got my first appointments scheduled for just a few days after we were to return to Pensacola. I was apprehensive about switching therapists. I liked my therapists in Birmingham and had gotten very comfortable with them. I was not looking forward to adjusting to new ones, but in just a few weeks, it would have to be done.

Back in Birmingham, therapy had been kicked into high gear. I was making some progress, especially with my right leg. It was getting much stronger, and while I did not have back my previous full range of motion in it, I did have enough of what they classified as functional range of motion. By the end of May, I could use my cane to walk short distances and to climb small flights of stairs. However, we were not having as much luck with my left leg. The progress in my range of motion had halted. I could get relatively decent extension, but on a good day, the most I could get my knee to flex or bend was to a 50-degree angle. We would often spend half of my therapy sessions working on knee flexion. Most days, I left therapy holding back tears from the pain of the sustained forced bending of my knee. However, some days I just could not hold them back, and they freely flowed down my cheeks while we pushed and pushed on my knee. Therapy on my elbow was going about the same, except I could not straighten or bend it. It was stuck. Right before we made the move to Pensacola, I would see my elbow surgeon to find out what was going on. I knew that I most likely would require another surgery and was not looking forward to that being confirmed.

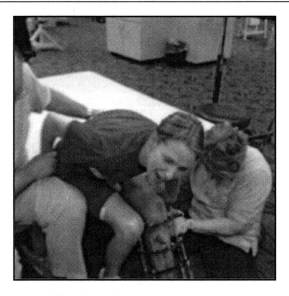

Working hard on bending my knee!

The trip to Pensacola was not the only trip we made during May. We also went back to Thomasville twice to visit friends and attend a couple of graduations. One of those weekends was my birthday. My parents and Michael did a lot to make that day special, but I have to admit that I had a little bit of a bad attitude as my birthday drew near. Not only would I not get to see Michael until we got to Thomasville that night, but I also would have to travel uncomfortably for five hours. On top of that, I would have therapy that day. However, underlying those frustrations was a bigger issue. In becoming a year older, I knew that I should be very grateful God had spared my life when it seemed I should not have made it. Instead, I struggled with both mental and spiritual battles. One, I did not want to live another year if, for the rest of my life, I would hurt so badly and be so confined in what I could do—I struggled with contentment. Two, I faced losing the opportunity to fulfill my childhood dream of becoming a nurse practitioner in the next year—I struggled with discouragement. Three, I was nowhere near where I had wanted to be in my recovery progress by my birthday—I struggled with perseverance. At that point in my recovery, I wrestled with physical, emotional, and spiritual brokenness. Facing my birthday brought a freshness to my struggles, all a result of the wrong focus, but nevertheless, these were the thoughts I battled with. Because God did spare my life as well as much of the quality of my life, I had finished another year of life and had the opportunity to begin journeying through another one. I faced a real decision: I could be dragged into the next year kicking and screaming in my heart and mind, or I could choose contentment. Really, it would not be just a one-time decision. Over the next several months, I would realize that I must daily and often hourly choose what my attitude would be. I could not control my circumstances, but I could control my attitude. As I moved back to Pensacola and into another year of life, I also moved into the next phase of my recovery, one wrought with emotional and spiritual battles as well as physical ones.

My Journal Entries:

5/12/12: For me to live is Christ and to die is gain!

What would you be willing to go through to be drawn closer to someone you love? Should we not do the same for Christ, who should be loved foremost in our lives?

Waiting patiently to be changed into a glorified image, changed to be like my Savior.

5/13/12: How can God be gracious and ordain such suffering in my life? But God is gracious because through our suffering we can become more like Him and experience Him in a more real way than we ever have. We become purified as gold is purified by fire, scaling off the unsightly dross from our lives and drawing us closer to being more like our Savior.

Many times, people will tell me I am lucky to be alive. That phrase always struck me as a little odd because quite frankly I did not feel so lucky. I wouldn't mind being in that perfect place called Heaven where there is no more pain, suffering, or tears, but instead God left me here to continually face pain, agony, and many tears. So, really, was I lucky or was I just chosen to suffer in this world a little longer? But still God has given me a wonderful opportunity to glorify my great, deserving God.

5/20/12: I can only accomplish great things by Him. I can only do His will by Him.

CHAPTER 6

Summer Battles

A day before we headed to Pensacola, I had an appointment with my elbow doctor. She was extremely thrilled to see me walk in with a cane. In fact, she was so excited that she called my leg surgeon to tell him how impressed she was with how I was doing. I personally thought that I needed to be much further along, but seeing her reaction served as an encouragement. She reminded me that even though I might not feel like it, I was much further along than most would be by this time. With my driven and determined personality, I tended to be much harder on myself than others would be, and while at times these qualities could be helpful, they could also be harmful. I needed to guard against discouragement. During the appointment, we did find out that I would have to have another elbow surgery. The surgeon explained that I had had significant bone growth that had overgrown in my elbow, and along with the hardware I had, it had frozen my joint. Although I would need to have the surgery done to have a functional arm, it did not have to be done immediately. To allow me to take a class and to begin working part-time for a semester, we decided to hold off on the surgery until

Christmas time. The appointment was not all bad news. I was finally given permission to stop taking my blood thinner injections. I hated those injections and was thrilled to finally be done with them!

Michael's Journal:

July 17: Julie has been recovering much faster than anyone expected. She was originally expected to not even walk or bear weight until the end of the year, but praise God she is now walking with minimal assistance!

June 2: Moving Day! It was finally time for me to go home! After being away for almost six months, it would be great to be back. I did not know when we left our house on December 17, 2011, that it would be the last time I would see it for almost six months. I remember thinking several times while in the hospital that I just wanted to go home. Moving day had taken a long time to arrive, but now it had come! And not only would I be home, but I would also get to have my puppy with me again! I had missed her so much and could not wait to have her with me! We had to bring a lot of equipment with us when we moved, and there was a lot to do to make sure I could get in the house. Pensacola Christian College, where my husband worked and where I had previously worked and would work for again, did so much to help us and to fix things around the house to make it more handicap-accessible. Jen had traveled from Birmingham with us and helped my mom unpack and organize all of the things we had brought from Birmingham. We had just the weekend before therapy would begin. I would miss Jen coming over every night to help with pin care and visit with me, but it would not be long before she to would move to Pensacola. She had taken a position on the faculty at the college, and I was excited for her to work there! She would be missed over the summer, but my sister would be arriving soon to help Mom in between the graduate classes she would be taking. The summer would be a busy one, but for me, it would seem to drag by as I waited and wondered what my future would hold.

June 4: First day of therapy at Andrews! I woke up feeling nervous. I hoped that I would like my therapists, since I would have to spend a lot of time with them, and I really did not want to dread seeing them as well as dread the therapy. I had gotten close to and trusted my therapists in Birmingham, and I knew it would be hard to adjust to new ones. I did not want therapists who would go easy on me, but I also did not want ones who did not want to invest time into helping me get better. I sat in my wheelchair in the waiting room, and I filled out all the paperwork. After just a few minutes, which seemed like an agonizing wait for me, my physical therapist, Stephen LaPlante, opened the door and escorted us back to his area. He introduced us to his Athletic Trainer, Ben Daughtery, whom we referred to as Red. He would also be working with me. Red greeted me with a handshake and a huge smile. He told me that over the next few months, we would all become close friends. I got the sense he really was serious about that, but I had my reservations. I was there to get a job done, not to make close friends, but what he said would stick in my mind during the coming months as I watched his prediction come true.

Me with my athletic trainer and physical therapist

After all the greetings, the initial evaluation began. I gave Stephen a brief summary of all the injuries I had sustained and what had been done so far in my recovery. As he finished my evaluation, he saw just how far we had to go and how much work it would require. We talked about exercises I needed to be doing at home and what we would be working towards in therapy. We would continue working on range of motion, but we also would start improving my core strength. Stephen told me we had a lot of work ahead but he was excited about it and would enjoy the challenge. Hearing this encouraged me that he would be invested in my recovery, but his demeanor intimidated me. I found myself at the end of the day hoping I would work more with Red than with him. As the summer passed though, I developed a great respect and appreciation for Stephen's knowledge and drive to help me recover, drastically changing my initial impression.

After physical therapy, it was on to hand therapy. I met Mary Ball, my hand therapist, whose creativity, positive attitude, knowledge, and encouragement were irreplaceable over the next year. She also saw that we would have a lot of work to do but was ready and eager for the challenge.

I left my first day of therapy feeling confident in my therapists and excited about working with them. These therapists that God put in my life were another amazing answer to our prayers. As we would see over the next year, they would not only be a source of pain, which was often the case, but they would also be a tremendous source of encouragement—and not just them, but the other therapists and trainers in the gym who also became invested in my recovery. I would leave on my last day of therapy with many more friends than I had started with.

My amazing therapy team!

Over the next two weeks, I worked hard at therapy, anxiously awaiting my next appointment with my leg doctor in Birmingham. He had said that we should be able to schedule the removal of my ex-fix during that next appointment. I was so ready for that thing to come off! I couldn't sleep well at night—the pin care was miserable, it made ranging my knee very difficult, and it was heavy! In addition, the doctor planned to manipulate my knee again so I could bend it more and not have to keep it extended out in front of me whenever I was sitting. We had been in the habit of bringing a tripod hunting stool with us wherever we went to support my left leg so I could sit down and rest from using my walker or cane. Pretty much everything would be at a standstill until I could get that contraption off. We all (family, therapists, and friends) hoped for good news at that appointment.

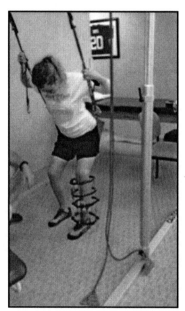

Working hard at physical therapy
anxiously awaiting getting the
external fixator off

June 15: Appointment day. I had been nauseous with anxiety about this appointment. So much rested on it. I hoped to spend the summer getting ready to start work and school in August and wanted to be more mobile so I could spend some time with my friends. A friend from Ohio, whom I had not seen in several years, was planning to visit in the coming weeks, and I wanted to be able to take her to the beach. That would not be possible with my ex-fix, so I really wanted good news. However, the minute the doctor walked into the room, I knew that something was not right. He had a serious, concerned look on his face. He said the ex-fix would not be able to come off. The bones at the top were healed, but the fractures at the bottom had not healed, and he was not sure when or if they would. He told us that he would wait one more month before we started discussing other options, but in the meantime, he wanted me to use a bone stimulator a couple of times every day. The rest of the conversation I didn't even hear as thoughts began to flood my mind. What did he mean by options? Was that his way of gently reminding me that amputation was still a possibility? After all these months of dealing with the pain and frustration of this ex-fix, would they still have to amputate??? I let my mind jump to the extremes, and in doing so, quickly slipped down the slippery slope into a deep discouragement. Over the next six weeks before my next appointment, I would fight and struggle through one of the toughest spiritual and emotional battles that I had encountered up to this point.

On the way home from Birmingham, I cried most of the way. Negatives thoughts inundated my mind. I kept asking God how He could do this to me. For so much of this struggle, I had kept my focus on Him and chosen not to be angry or bitter, but now would He allow the possibility of amputation because my leg would not heal? How could He do that to me? I was hurt and losing the battle against anger and bitterness. I felt discouraged thinking that the suffering I had gone through the last few months might be for nothing. Loneliness began to set in, and I felt as if no one would understand the emotions and pain I had experienced! Even if they could, I had no idea how to express it to them. I had felt this loneliness many times before, but this time it was amplified. Before, I had at least been able to talk to God about it, knowing He already knew what I was going through—but not this time. This time, I was angry with Him. I did not want to talk to Him about it because I blamed Him for it! I would spend nights lying in bed feeling uncomfortable, staring at the ceiling, and fighting with Him over allowing this. The frustration and discouragement wore on me. I hated facing each new day and often wished that I just had not made it through the accident. I struggled desperately with spiritual and emotional brokenness. Even though I would often put on a smile for others, inside I was in turmoil and was throwing one major pity party. But God was not through with me yet. He still loved me, regardless of my actions, and He faithfully continued to prove that to me.

My Journal Entries:

6/17/12: Just a bunch of jumbled thoughts in my head. I am having such a hard time working through them all. I feel as if I am losing the battle in my head. I have been as patient as I can, more so than I ever thought I could be. I have been willing to have a good attitude and make the most out of this trial. It is so hard and discouraging for my last two appointments to have negative news. My back and ankles kill me, I am tired of sitting all the time, and now there is no end in sight. So...I am struggling. I know that God knows best, that He is in control and aware of the situation, and that He loves me. But how could He allow such discouraging news when He knows how tired and discouraged I am? My mind wants to trick me into believing that He is cruel and uncaring. How could He strip away my life— my job, my grad work, my marriage, my enjoyment in exercise, and my ability to play the piano and guitar? But, I know that is all untrue. I just can't convince my heart to accept it, so I struggle day and night. It really is an exhausting battle in my mind. I strive to keep my mind busy to avoid meditating on things too much because inevitably I will lose the battle. I really think victory over this struggle is far beyond me. I must continue to pray for God to change my carnal heart in its tendency towards bitterness, resentment, and depression. It cannot be conquered by my will. My carnal heart continuously pesters me with thoughts such as not deserving all that has happened and how cruel it is that God forces me to be in this trial so long. But my heart, which knows that these things and this thinking are absurd, fights against it. My flesh is so strong though! Only through God's intervention can my carnal cravings be defeated. Perhaps God has allowed this trial to be prolonged so that I may more effectively and passionately share about all that has taken place physically and spiritually, or maybe someone still needs to see me in the midst of my trial. Most definitely it's because He still has much to teach me.

6/24/12: Michael still often calls me his princess. I always cringe when he does that now because I do not feel like that at all. A princess is supposed to be beautiful, without blemishes and scars from head to toe. How am I ever supposed to feel like a princess when my body is so deformed? Michael first called me his princess before my body was so disfigured, but now I don't feel as if I deserve that term of endearment. As I was thinking about this the other night, I was suddenly struck with the realization that my situation mirrored another amazing concept. Essentially, I really am a princess because I am a child of the King. However there is a small but amazing difference in the circumstances, because Michael chose me to be his princess when I wasn't scarred and broken, but Christ chose me to be His princess seeing what a dirty, filthy, and imperfect human being I was. What an amazing example of God's unconditional love for us sinful human beings.

In the middle of this pity party I threw for myself, my friend Alyssa came to visit. She was just what I needed. We enjoyed catching up, laughed a lot, and stayed busy with therapy and preparing for the party we were going to have for the Fourth of July. Alyssa also helped my mom with work around the house and with taking care of me. Her energy and laughter were contagious and helped me start to get over my pity party.

During this time, my brother Jon, his wife Jess, and their two children, JJ and Georgia, also had come for a visit. They had moved back to the United States from Africa at the beginning of June and now lived only a couple of hours away. All of these visitors really helped to encourage me. We had a wonderful Fourth of July party, organized by my sister. Several of my friends came over, and we enjoyed just hanging out together celebrating. This week of reprieve and distractions had been just what I needed. I truly believe God sent Alyssa and the others at just the right time to give me the encouragement I needed to help me see things from a different perspective—even when I least deserved it.

Enjoying spending time with my niece
and nephew!

The encouragement came at just the right time. Just a week after Alyssa left, I was asked to speak at a Ladies' Conference and share my testimony. During the past few weeks, I had struggled as to how I would be able to do that when I had so much undealt-with anger and bitterness. Shortly after Alyssa left, I had another one of those nighttime conversations with God, but this time instead of anger, it was simply discouragement that I talked with Him about. That night, as I lay there crying after baring my heart to Him, God brought to my mind this fact: He had spared my life, spared my mind, met absolutely every need we had had since the accident, and given me grace to face absolutely every challenge with strength and confidence. If He had taken care of me through all those things, why on earth would I doubt His ability to do the same thing with just my leg! Even if it did need to be amputated, I would still be able to learn how to walk. I still would not have to spend the rest of my life in a wheelchair, and

He would give me the same grace He had already abundantly poured out on me to deal with whatever He chose to allow into my life. So why was I refusing to trust Him? Perhaps He needed to challenge me again to grow my faith, or perhaps He wanted to use me in a way that would be more effective if I still had the ex-fix on or had an amputated leg. Whatever His purpose or plan was, that night, through what seemed like almost an audible conversation with God, I came to grips with what was going on with my leg. I gave whatever happened over to Him and trusted that He would give me grace.

Just a week before my next appointment, I sat on a stage, ex-fix and all, at the Ladies' Conference and shared my "Grace Story" with them. I shared with complete confidence in my God and His ability to heal my leg or to give grace for whatever the next step would be. As I shared my story, I was again reminded of all God had done in my life over the past few months, and the reminder served to strengthen my resolve to trust Him even further. The ladies whom I shared with at that conference not only got to see God's grace through my past, but they got to see His grace actively working in me. They saw my battered physical condition and heard what was on my heart after walking out of one of the deepest spiritual struggles I had battled through, and they joined me in praying for miraculous healing.

July 23: Back to Birmingham once again for another doctor's appointment. It was the long-awaited day, but surprisingly, my mind felt at peace. Sure, I hoped for good news, but I knew whatever the outcome was, I would be okay. First stop was for X-rays. This time was the first time that they were not unbearably painful. They took several views, called the doctor to look at them, and then came back to retake the films again. I wondered why they had to repeat them. I tried not to get my hopes up but thought that maybe he just wanted to be sure it really had healed. I quickly pushed the thought away as we went to wait in the room for the doctor. A few minutes later, my doctor walked in with one of the biggest smiles on his face that I had ever seen. He tapped me on the ex-fix, looked at me, and said, "Are you ready to get this thing off?" A cheer went up in the room as my mom, dad, and husband all celebrated this news with me. The doctor laughed and told us that he could not believe it, but it had healed! He enjoyed the moment with us and explained what would take place during the surgery. Then he sent us to schedule the surgery and get everything done that needed to be completed before the morning of the surgery. As we waited for all of these things to be done, we sent out messages over Facebook and to all our friends and family who had prayed so hard for this result. This was a specific answer to many specific prayers that had gone up over the past few weeks! I could not wait to get back to tell my therapists. They had really been hoping for good results so we could continue our progress! I would have one more day of therapy before my surgery on Friday, and then finally I would be free of my cage!

The next day of therapy, I decided to have some fun with Stephen and Red. I walked in with a discouraged looked on my face. Red met me in the hallway before reaching the therapy gym and asked me how the appointment had gone. I looked at him and said, "Well, the doctor says I have to wait until Friday to take it off!" Red broke into a huge smile and gave me a hug. He was just as excited as we were. I did the same thing to Stephen when I got to his tables, and he was very relieved and excited to hear the news also. Finally, we could hopefully make some progress with my walking.

July 27: Surgery day again! But that morning, it was all smiles for me! The day had finally come! My ex-fix was going to come off.

Even with the pain that I knew would follow the surgery, I still could not wait for it to happen. We got to the hospital and I got ready to go back to surgery. When one of the residents came to see me before the surgery, I told him that I really wanted to keep my ex-fix and asked him to see whether that would be possible. He said that usually it was not allowed, but he would check for me. After all, we did pay for it and it had been a part of me for quite a while. Unfortunately, they could not give it to me. That was a little disappointing but was not going to ruin that day for me.

Once again, they had to put in a block, and of course, I remembered every uncomfortable moment of it. By this time, I had gotten fairly used to it. I knew that later on, the uncomfortableness would be worth the pain relief it would provide. In a short while, my leg would be free from its cage and much, much lighter. These were the last things I thought as I drifted off to sleep. Over the next couple of hours, they removed my ex-fix, cleaned out and scraped the extra scar tissue and bone from around my knee, and ranged my knee. After all of this was completed, they placed my leg in a cast and then hooked me up to another CPM. This time, it would be vital that I keep that knee moving so it would not freeze up again. As soon as the surgery was completed, they rolled me out to post-op for a short time and then up to my room. When I rolled into the room, I saw my mother- and father-in-law, who had come to visit their children and to go to Michael's graduation the following week. It was good to see them, especially for Michael, who also needed some encouragement during this time. However, the excitement of the surgery did not last long, and we began to face several months of problems.

For some reason, my right arm itched a lot and felt like it was burning. I looked down and saw big red, raised welts ascending up my arm. Immediately, I realized that I had just used my patient-controlled pain pump, which had administered morphine into the IV catheter that was in that arm. The hives had come up right after I had pushed the pain button. It looked like I was having an allergic reaction to the morphine. I pointed out the hives to the nurse, and she said that they did not have any other pain medication to give me then, so I should probably just keep using the morphine. Perhaps I was one of those terror patients at this point in time, but what she said really frustrated me. I held up my arm and pointed to the welts that now covered my arm and said, "I have hives from the morphine. I don't think it is a good idea for me to keep using this medication." She looked at me as she turned to leave and told me that she did not know how long it would be before they could get more pain medication. It did end up being quite a while before she brought anything else in, but at least something else had been ordered.

That was not the only problem that night. As I started settling in for the night, I started to intensely itch all over, most likely from the pain medication I had received. My mom called the nurses' station and told them I was itching and asked whether I could get some Benadryl, which of course would have to be ordered by the doctor. I knew this would take some time, so we also asked for some washcloths in the meantime. At least maybe a cool, wet washcloth would help alleviate the intenseness of the itch. An hour later, nothing had happened. My mom went out to the nurses' station and asked whether she could just go herself and get a washcloth. She was told that someone would have to bring it in, and they would be there soon. An hour later, still no one had come. Thankfully, by then shift change had come. When the new nurse came in, we asked her for a wash-cloth, and she immediately got one for us. She also apologized that it had taken so long, and within just a few minutes, she brought me some Benadryl and had it infusing through my IV. The rest of the night was better, as she came to check on me often and took really good care of me.

The next day, I saw the doctor, and he told me that for a few days I could not put weight on my leg. That meant back to the wheel-chair for me. Even if he had not said that, I think I would have had to use the wheelchair anyway. My pain still was not under control from my time without pain medication on the day before, and gen-erally overall, I did not feel well. However, time was of the essence with bending my knee. I could not slack off, and I needed to work hard on it.

This hospital stay did not last long, and within just a few days, we were back in Pensacola and back to therapy. On the first day back at therapy, I knew I looked terrible. I could barely hold my head up and was very weak and pale; however, there was work to be done, and I needed to go to therapy. Once I got up on the table, we were anxious to see how well my knee would bend after having it ranged. We all were excited to see that I could get it just a little bit past 90 degrees. That was much better than what it had been, but I still had a long way to go. That day we worked some on stretching it, but not much more than that. I was too weak and needed some recovery time.

Unfortunately, as the days went on, my pain did not improve, and I continued to be reminded of my unrelenting physical brokenness. I had difficulty walking in the cast, experienced tremendous pain in my lower leg and ankle, and could not sleep at night because of the pain of leaving my leg in the CPM. Every time I would put my leg back in the CPM, tears would come as it painfully stretched my already sore, tight muscles. We did eventually get a different type of medication for the pain, which helped some, but still, something did not seem right. My doctor in Birmingham had me see one of the doctors in Pensacola. He took the cast off, X-rayed my leg, and put the cast back on. This revealed no definitive answer for why the pain was so bad. Perhaps it was just the cast. The new cast did help some, but I still had a lot of pain in my lower leg and ankle. I hoped that maybe at my next appointment with my doctor in Birmingham, they could take the cast off and put me in a walking boot. At least I could take the walking boot off for showers and for aquatic therapy. My therapist really wanted me to get onto the treadmill in the pool. They hoped that would really improve my ability to walk, but until I could get out of the cast, that could not happen.

The onslaught of frustrations continued as just two days after dealing with my leg, I ended up in the ER with nausea, vomiting, and extreme pain. I once again had a kidney stone, and I required fluids for rehydration. This time, they referred me to a kidney doctor to address the kidney stones, which were now becoming frequent events. As if I did not already have enough doctors to see!

August 13: It was back to Birmingham to see my leg doctor again. I hoped to get some answers for what had been going on. During the past few days, the pain in my leg had improved some, but it still bothered me. The doctor came in and said that my leg had two spots that still needed some additional healing, but he felt that a walking boot would enable me to walk better on that leg and put weight through my leg to encourage healing. He also wanted me to continue using the bone stimulator until the next appointment. At least the cast would come off and stay off! The walking boot was much easier to walk in, and I could not wait to try out the pool at therapy!

Things started to get busy that next week. I started my last graduate class before clinicals started, I started work, and I went to therapy for two hours three times a week. Before the wreck, I had been working towards getting my M.S.N., with a concentration as a family nurse practitioner. Because of having to delay my graduate work, I had to add an extra course to my plan of study to be able to graduate. It was not too difficult a course, and it allowed me to get back into the swing of graduate school. I still did not know whether I would be able to start my clinicals in January, but I wanted to be ready just in case I could. If I did not start them then, I would have to repeat most of the courses I had already taken, because too much time would have elapsed between starting and graduation. Originally, my doctors and others had doubted that I could get back to graduate school by then but encouraged me to make the attempt. I still had a long way to go, and things were not going in my favor.

Starting back to work helped keep me distracted and served as a significant encouragement to me. It helped me get back into a routine and allowed me to put my focus on something other than my circumstances. Pensacola Christian College did so much for my husband and me during that time. They offered to give me my job back and patiently waited until I knew for sure that I could work. Once I started work, the Chair of Nursing worked with me to coordinate my work with therapy schedules and doctor appointments. It was such a blessing to work for a place that cared so much for me and for my recovery. Going back to work with the faculty was like going home to my family. The love and support they gave truly made a difference.

The first week back to work, school, and therapy went pretty well; however, by the weekend, I was exhausted and in pain. I hoped that within the next few weeks, the pain would improve, but unfortunately, that was not the case. I did finally get into the pool at therapy, but it did not really improve my walking as we had hoped. In fact, every night after therapy, my leg and ankle would hurt so much that I could barely put weight on it. As the weeks passed, I eventually got to the point where I could barely put weight on it at all. During the appointment with my leg doctor early in September, he told me that he wanted me to see a foot and ankle specialist in Pensacola and that he also wanted an MRI done of my ankle. After the MRI, the doctor discovered I had a stress fracture in my left ankle and would need to stay off of my foot for a while. Since I was starting my job, I had to have a way to get around. After talking with my therapist, I decided to try out a knee walker. We purchased a pretty red one, and it was actually kind of fun to cruise around on. At the same time, though, it also meant that things were not progressing as they should. I began to worry that I would never walk again without an assistive device and that I would never get to finish my schooling to become a nurse practitioner. These thoughts plagued my mind at night and prevented me from getting the rest I needed.

During the middle of September, we started taking the students to the hospital for their clinicals. The Chair of Nursing had placed me on the same floor as one of my good friends, Lindsey Scott, so she could watch out for me and help me get around. The two days we spent each week at the hospital were long but kept me busy. Lindsey would pick me up around 5 a.m., and once I was in the car, she would pick up my heavy knee walker and put it in the trunk. Then, once we arrived at the hospital, she would get it out again for me and help me up to my designated spot on the floor. During the clinical days, I would do all of the written work, grading, and med quizzes with the students and help out with whatever else the instructors needed. Lindsey would drop me off back at home around 5 p.m., and by then, I was usually exhausted. Thankfully, my mom was able to stay through the fall semester to help with the things I still could not do, such as fixing my hair, getting in and out of the shower, cooking, and cleaning. Especially on these clinical days, she would have supper ready for us when I got home. It was a big help that she stayed because Michael worked full-time, and he could not take me to and from therapy. In addition to everything else, my mom was my chauffeur too!

The first day of clinicals arrived, and I woke up extremely nauseated, with an all-too-familiar sharp pain in my back. I tried to ignore it and started getting ready anyway, but soon I started feeling sicker and the pain became unbearable. I had another kidney stone! I ended up missing my first day of clinicals with the students! The kidney stones had become a very frustrating nuisance.

When I finally got in to see the urologist, he discovered that not only did I have a kidney stone, but I also had a bladder infection. The urologist told me I had to drink more water and then recommended a supplement for me to start taking. He said that it would take a couple of months for the supplement to take effect but that if I would keep taking it, along with drinking more water, it should help to prevent the stones. I knew I needed to drink more water, but I just hated to do so because as a result I would have to urinate. It was very difficult and often painful mobility-wise to do this, so I had avoided drinking a lot of liquids. Now that would have to change. I had two more bouts with kidney stones over the next two months, but the increase in water and the supplements eventually did help prevent more kidney stones from occurring.

By the end of September, I needed some encouragement. I had had a lot of bad news and a lot of frustrating things had happened during the past month. Michael and I just needed to get away for a special weekend. For most of my life, I had always wanted to go to a Georgia Bulldogs game. I had been born near Athens, Georgia, and had lived in Georgia all of my life and with my older brothers had grown up watching the Dawgs play football every fall. It was a dream of mine to go to one of their games. Now my brother- and sister-in-law were making that dream a possibility. They lived not too far away from the university and bought us tickets to go to a game with them. It was wonderful! We had such a good time, and it was exactly what Michael and I had needed. We had quite a bit of alone time as we traveled to and from Georgia. Time alone had been a rarity for us in the past year, and this trip allowed us to have that much-needed time. In addition to the awesome experience we had watching the Georgia game, we also got to visit with family and their church, who had prayed so much for us. Once again, God had provided for us by bringing along just the perfect encouragement to help us continue fighting through this trial.

Excited to go to a Georgia game!

My Journal Entries:

9/30/12: Initially, when I first came to, I had a calm, confident assurance that God had chosen this trial for me for a reason. The peace and confidence I had in that are indescribable and supernatural. Now, several months later, the strong confidence and assurance are gone. In my mind, I know it is truth, but my heart is reluctant to accept it. Why is it that my heart no longer wants to accept the truth? God has not changed. His ultimate goal is for my good. How hard it is to keep my heart humble and accepting of God's sovereignty. What a difficult spiritual battle I must face on a minute-by-minute basis. God is still good, God is still sovereign, and He still has a purpose for my life, for this trial, and for my struggles.

The month of October proved to be a difficult month. I had hit a brick wall in therapy. There seemed to be no reason that I should not be able to walk, but I could not. I remember one particular day at therapy that I asked Stephen what he thought was going on and whether I ever would be able to walk without an assistive device again. Stephen knew what was at stake in relation to my grad school and knew how hard I had worked to get ready to start grad school clinicals. He had me walk as best as I could, while focusing on all the things he had taught me to think about when trying to walk. I felt pain in each step I took and felt the abnormal gait. No matter how hard I tried, it would not improve. After I finished walking some for him, I sat back on the table and looked at him for his opinion. He did not have to say much. I could see it on his face. Something was not right, but nobody could figure out what was causing the problems. With all the work I had put in, I should be much further along, but if anything, I was losing ground. I valued and trusted Stephen's opinion, and with what I saw that day, I knew my dreams for starting back into the nurse practitioner program were slowly fading. I walked out of therapy desperately trying to hold back my tears. As I climbed into the van, I couldn't hold them back any longer. The discouragement and hopelessness that I had been feeling for a while came pouring out as the tears flooded down my cheeks. My mom put my knee walker in the trunk and walked around to the driver's side of the van. As she got in, I heard a knock on my window and looked over to see Stephen standing there. Embarrassed that he had seen me crying, I rolled down my window to talk to him. First of all, he offered me one of the chocolate-covered strawberries he held in his hand, which in my opinion would make any person feel better, and then he looked at me and told me not to give up, that we would figure out a way, whatever it took, to get me walking by January. While I still had my doubts about grad school, it meant a lot to me that he took the time to encourage me. Knowing how invested he and Red were in getting me walking again helped me to keep focused, even with the setbacks. In my opinion, I truly had the best therapists ever!

October also brought bad news regarding my elbow. Without surgery, it would remain locked at 90 degrees and I could not make much progress with it. Surgery had been scheduled for early in December with my elbow doctor in Birmingham, but in October we found out that the doctor would be moving from Birmingham in November, which meant that I would have to find a different doctor. My hand therapist, Mary, recommended a doctor there at Andrews Institute whom she thought could really do a great job with my elbow. I called to try to set up an appointment, and at first, I was told he might not be able to take me. Mary talked with the office staff, and eventually she helped me to get an appointment with him. She was amazing! She always was quick to help, quick to encourage, and very knowledgeable about what was going on with my arm. She even helped to make the flap on my leg look a little better. Many times, just for fun, she would decorate the wrap I had to keep over the flap with different holiday decorations. She made things like stars for the Fourth of July and a Christmas tree for Christmas. She knew how to take a rough situation and make it fun. Her encouragement and friendship meant so much to me. I could always count on her to help me out whenever I needed it, including finding a surgeon for my elbow.

The first appointment I had with the elbow surgeon was a good one. Dr. Callahan took the time to show me and explain to me what was going on with my elbow. He explained what he hoped to accomplish during the surgery and what the recovery would be like afterwards. I was very glad Mary had recommended him. We were able once again to schedule the surgery for early in December, right after I would complete my graduate class for the semester.

At the end of October, I had two more appointments. One with my plastic surgeon and one with the foot and ankle specialist. During my appointment with the plastic surgeon, he told me that I had a hernia on my left lower leg that could be fixed, but he did not want to fix it until he figured out what was wrong with my leg. He thought that something was definitely wrong and that most likely, I would have to have surgery again. Hopefully, we would find out for sure the next day at my appointment with the foot and ankle specialist in Pensacola.

As I went to the appointment the following day, I was very nervous. So much rested on what the doctor would say, and unfortunately, the news was as bad as I had feared it would be. The doctor told me my leg had healed wrong and, as a result, was causing the severe pain I had. He said they would need to rebreak my leg and put it back in the ex-fix for a few months. The recovery would be around three months at the least, and because of my flap, he did not feel comfortable doing the procedure. He offered to consult with my doctor in Birmingham to let him know what he thought was going on. Of course, that would mean more waiting to find out what the doctor in Birmingham thought.

After the appointment, I was sick with disappointment. I had thought I was done with the ex-fix, my "archenemy", and not only that, if what he had predicted was true, there would be no way I could start back to grad school. In just one appointment, my world came quickly crashing down around me as the reality of my physical brokenness once again took priority in my thoughts. I think perhaps this was another one of the most difficult emotional times during my recovery. I had to come to grips with the fact that I probably would not be able to finish grad school, even after all of the hard work I had put in over the past year. I also had to face having that awful ex-fix back on my leg for several months! After the appointment, we went down to see my therapists and tell them the news. The discouragement was obvious on my face—a definite change from normal, since I had a reputation there for always smiling, even if they were causing me pain. That day and the next few days of therapy, there were no smiles as I struggled to come to grips with losing my dream of becoming a nurse practitioner and struggled with my emotional brokenness. However, I could always count on my therapy friends to encourage me. A few days after my appointment, I received a bouquet of chocolate-covered fruit from Edible Arrangements with an encouraging card from all my friends at therapy! This was another reminder that I had a whole team of people cheering me on—just what I needed to put a smile back on my face. As I have said, this was the best therapy group ever!

Encouragement from my friends at therapy!

The next week, I finally received a phone call from my doctor in Birmingham. He told me that he did not think putting the ex-fix back on would be the best option and that he wanted me to come back to Birmingham and get a standing X-ray done. He told me that he would look at the films, consult with some of the other surgeons there, and then get back with me. By the time we got to Birmingham to have the films taken, the first week of November was already over. If I needed to have surgery, my recovery time afterwards before having to start grad school was quickly disappearing. I anxiously awaited the phone call from my leg surgeon, knowing that with each day that passed, I was losing valuable time. Finally, on Tuesday of the next week, the surgeon called and said that he thought the best thing to do would be to break my leg in two places and put a rod down it. He knew we were pressed for time and scheduled my surgery for that Thursday. I was relieved to finally have surgery scheduled and to hear that no ex-fix would be involved! Now the question would be how quickly could I recover. I would have just a month and a half to be walking without assistance. It was a task that in my eyes seemed impossible.

November 15: It was back to the OR again. This surgery brought a lot of nerves, frustration, and dread. I dreaded the pain that would follow, and I dreaded the intense therapy that I knew would have to take place after the surgery. I also dreaded that my worst fears would be confirmed and that this surgery would not fix the pain and I still would not be able to walk. These thoughts consumed my mind as I drifted off to sleep.

What was wrong with my leg? I groaned as I woke up to intense pain, so intense that I could barely breathe. My leg felt like it was on fire and being ripped off all at the same time! Tears began to roll down my face, and everything around me was a blur. I tried to focus on what was going on as I heard one of the hospital personnel ask whether the block had been started. Suddenly, there was a rush of people checking to see whether the medication had been started for my block. The medication had been placed into the pump, but the pump had never been started. I had come out of surgery with absolutely no pain medication! No wonder the pain was so intense! It took a few minutes for the block to take effect, and in the meantime, they had to put another block in to make sure my whole leg had relief. To do this, they had to roll me over, which, with the pain I was already in, hurt tremendously. They began looking for the right place to place the block. I stayed on my side for over half an hour as they poked and prodded my buttocks trying to find the right spot. Finally, the surgeon came over, not happy with what he saw and not happy with what he had found out about the block not being started at the appropriate time. He told them to get the best person they could to start the block immediately. He then walked around to where I could see him and said that he needed to apologize. He went on to explain that when they opened up my leg to do the osteotomy, my bone moved! One of the fractures had never healed! For the last three months, I had been walking on a broken leg! He said he was sorry that it had taken so long to catch it, since it would have been an easy fix that could have been taken care of months ago, but the X-rays had not shown that the fracture still existed. Several skilled orthopedic surgeons had looked at my films, but they had just not shown any evidence of a fracture. He said that when he saw it during the surgery, he could not believe it, but it would actually work in our favor regarding my recovery time. They only had to break my bone in one place so they could get the rod down, and he told me that he wanted me to put weight through the leg immediately. I could barely wait. I had a feeling things were going to be better. This just had to work.

After I thought about what my surgeon had told me about my bone still being fractured, it made a lot of sense. I had actually told my mom and my therapist several times that I wondered if the bone was still broken. Often when I would put weight on the leg, it felt like my bone would shift, and at times it felt like it popped or clicked. I had had a hard time balancing on that leg, despite working really hard to improve it—no wonder it had hurt so bad to put weight on it. In a way, I was relieved. Knowing there was still a fracture at least validated the pain I had been complaining about.

The next day, I felt weak and exhausted, and as I had expected, I needed blood again. Because I was receiving blood, the therapist could not come work with me in the morning. It actually disappointed me because I looked forward to getting up for the first time and my doctor had said I had to get up that day. The therapists had said they would be back in the afternoon, but as nighttime approached, they still had not come. I was tired of waiting, so of course I decided that I did not need them to get up. We had my gait belt and my dad and Michael were there, so I thought it shouldn't be a problem. I really wanted to get up. So I did, and the minute my foot hit the floor, I knew something was different. My leg felt balanced, it felt right, and I felt like I could put weight on it! A smile spread across my face. I was going to be able to walk again! I used my cane to walk to the hospital room door and back a few times and then got back in bed, excited to see the therapists in the morning.

The next morning, the therapists came, and they set a goal for me to walk up and down my hospital wing. I soon reached that goal and was not ready to stop so we kept walking all around the hospital floor. It felt wonderful! It finally felt normal to walk! Sure, there was some pain with it, mostly due to the tightness of my Achilles tendon, but with some stretching, eventually that would get better.

After several days in the hospital, I was finally dismissed to go home. The next few weeks were going to be busy. Not only did I need to put all my energy into my therapy, but also Thanksgiving week was coming up, as well as the first court hearing with the girl who had hit us. For Thanksgiving, we went to Georgia for a few days before heading over to Troy, Alabama, for the court hearing. We enjoyed getting to spend time with my brother Jon and his family, celebrating all that we had to be thankful for, especially over the past year, and, of course, eating a lot of food! The next week would be an emotional one, and we needed this relaxation.

November 27: The first court date had arrived. This would be the first time that I would see the girl who had hit us. The court would be deciding whether she would be tried as a minor or as an adult. Because she was under 21 and alcohol was involved, being tried as a minor was a possibility. I had some concerns about the hearing. Up until then, choosing to forgive her for all she had done had been easy, but now that I would be able to put a face with the name, I worried that it might make things more difficult. Also, I had no idea what would be said or how it would be said. I did not know how I would respond to discussing the accident and what I had gone through in much detail, especially since I would be the one to have to relay it when I took the stand.

I felt uncomfortable entering the courtroom, feeling the stares of people looking at my deformed leg as I hobbled into the room. I was not looking forward to it, but at least after the hearing, we planned to meet with some of the rescue personnel who had helped save my life. That gave me something to look forward to and something else to focus on. Finally, the court was called into session. God gave strength through the next hour as I testified and listened to the girl and some of her family do the same. By the end of the court session, even the defendant was speechless with the gravity and difficulty of my situation. I think most of us left the courtroom that day with a relative surety that the judge would rule in our favor. We found out later that day that he had and sometime in the coming spring, she would be tried as an adult.

That night we had the opportunity to meet with a few of the people who had been a part of rescuing us. After the emotionally draining day, I needed some encouragement. We enjoyed sitting and talking with several of the men. They told us their memories of the accident, and we talked about what a miracle it was that I had come so far. One of the men I got to meet was the lieutenant fireman who had been on the scene. He had been responsible for coordinating our rescue. As we began to talk, I mentioned that I was frustrated with my progress and that I wondered whether I would ever get to be a nurse practitioner. That triggered a conversation about what had happened in his life. Before he became a fireman, he had been in an accident and had had procedures similar to mine. Unfortunately, unlike my case, they could not save his lower leg, and he had to have an amputation of the bottom part of his leg, requiring him to have a prosthesis. Everyone had told him that because of that, he would never be able to be a fireman like he wanted, but with hard work and determination, he did become one. Not only that, he also became a lieutenant. Amazing! It was just what I needed to hear! Here was someone else who understood. He had been through a similar circumstance and still had reached his seemingly impossible dream. Hearing his story strengthened my determination and drive to start clinicals by January, and I decided to go ahead and take the step to register and pay for my classes as soon as I could when we got home. It was yet another encouragement that God placed in my path to let me know He was still there walking with me and giving me strength to accomplish His will.

Enjoyed getting to meet the firemen who helped
save my life!

Just three weeks after my leg surgery, it was back to the OR, this time in the outpatient setting. The elbow surgeon planned to take out the hardware in my elbow and clean out bone fragments. The surgery would be less than two hours, and following the surgery, they would leave me on a pain pump, which should keep my arm relatively numb for the first few days. I had never had an arm surgery that had not been severely painful, so I was really hoping this time would be different. Unfortunately, that would not be the case.

December 4th: As I woke up that morning, my mom told me that my sister-in-law was in labor. Of all the days for the baby to come, it would be the day I was to have my surgery! We had said all along that it would probably happen and sure enough it did! I hated that my mom could not be present for the birth, but I was very thankful that she was there with me. I could not wait to get the surgery completed. I was tired of not being able to move my arm. It had made things like eating and getting dressed very difficult. Hopefully, this would be the last surgery for a while!

We arrived at the surgery center and checked in, and eventually I was taken back to get prepped for the surgery. This time, after they sedated me to put the block in, I only remembered being rolled into the OR, and then after what seemed just a few minutes, I was out again.

I woke up from surgery with a rather large, uncomfortable, bulky splint on my arm. I could tell that by the time I got that thing off, we would not be friends. Not too long after waking up, I got up into a wheelchair and was wheeled to meet my parents and Michael at the front of the surgery center. Before leaving, I was handed all the metal that had been taken out of my arm. I could not believe how much had been in there! As I was rolled out, my mom told me that I had a new nephew and that everyone was doing well. My surgery had been successful, but there had been some complications that would result in a longer, more painful recovery. Originally, they had hoped to use a triceps-sparing approach to accomplish what needed to be done, but eventually, they had to cut the triceps to get the job accomplished. This was not what we had hoped for but at least the surgery had been successful and positive results were expected. We would just have to be patient and careful with the triceps as we gave it the time it needed to heal. Now, I would not only have physical therapy to focus on, but as soon as the splint came off, I would have hand therapy too.

The block effectively kept my arm numb until late that evening. As the initial block wore off, I began to experience excruciating pain. I had not expected the pain to be so severe because theoretically the pain pump should have numbed most of the pain, but that was not the case. I thought that if I could go to sleep, maybe the pain would improve, but sleep evaded me as the pain continued to rapidly increase in severity. Apparently, this elbow surgery would be like all the others and cause tremendous pain. I cannot even begin to adequately describe how awful the pain felt. It felt like my arm was being both sawed off and burned off at the same time. I did not sleep a bit that night. We called the anesthesiologist to see what could be done, and he had me begin taking pain medicine. When the pain did not improve, they increased the dose.

Over the next few days, the pain gradually decreased but still made me extremely uncomfortable. We came to the conclusion that the pain pump had not been effective, since I had full function and feeling in the fingers that it was supposed to be keeping numb. Nights were the hardest—with the splint, it was nearly impossible to get comfortable enough to fall asleep. Almost my entire arm had been splinted, and it had been splinted in extension. The top of the cast cut into the sensitive skin of my upper arm and the tightness of it was annoying. Of course, it needed to be tight, but that did not change how frustrating it was to be so uncomfortable. I could not wait to get the splint off! I would have to wait a week though, and by the time that week was over, I was ready to be done with it. My shoulders and neck hurt from the weight of the splint, and it really got in the way. The appointment date we had been given was for exactly one week from the surgery date. When we arrived at the office, we found out that they had accidentally scheduled me for the wrong date and that the surgeon was in surgery that day. If I had really thought about it, I could have figured that out before going all the way to the office, but I had not. When we figured out the mistake, I was devastated! I think the lack of sleep, the pain, and the frustration the splint had caused just all hit me. I fought to hold back tears as we walked from the office. It would be only two more days, but I was so tired of it. Thankfully, after the next day, the splint finally came off, and it was time to get serious about getting that elbow moving.

Directly after my appointment, I went to see my hand therapist. My elbow, of course, was very stiff, but she walked me through the exercises that I would need to do faithfully over the next few weeks to get my elbow moving. She had been able to watch my surgery and told me more about the obstacles the doctor had run into and how he had successfully worked around them to get my elbow fixed. I was fortunate to have the surgeon and the hand therapist I had. With some hard work, I should get good function out of my arm.

It was now nearly mid-December, which meant it had been almost a year since the accident. It had been a long year, but a year in which we had seen God work in so many miraculous ways. Even though I wished I was much further along in my recovery by this point in time, my doctors and therapists often reminded me that I was much further along than most others in my situation would be. The coming year would be full of very different battles but would still be full of evidence of God's miraculous, beautiful grace.

CHAPTER 7

Strength For The Impossible

The last part of December was focused on strenuous therapy. I worked hard to do exactly as Stephen and Mary said, patiently enduring the pain as we pushed to get my joints moving and faithfully doing my exercises and stretching at home. Working with my elbow tended to be the most painful of all of my joints. I would often sit at the hand table with my head turned to the side, sometimes successfully and sometimes unsuccessfully trying to hold back tears as we placed sustained pressure on the joint to get it into flexion or extension. My therapists and I all worked hard to make progress. A week before New Year's, Stephen looked at me and asked me when I was going to get rid of the cane. Up until that point, I had thought that for balance reasons, I really needed the cane. My limp without the cane was severe, and I wore out quickly when I was not using it. His comment surprised me, but I knew I needed to start preparing myself to get rid of it. He told me that my New Year's resolution needed to be never using my cane again. That week he made me do most of my exercises without my cane. His comment stuck in my mind as something to work towards.

During Christmas break, we did a lot of traveling. We went to Georgia for my mom's birthday and for Christmas Day, and then we came went back to Pensacola for a few days of therapy. After that, we traveled down to Lakeland, Florida, to visit my grandparents and aunts and uncles for a couple of days and then back to Georgia for New Year's Day. Before going to bed on New Year's Eve, I placed my cane away from my bed since I would not be using it the next morning when I got up.

On New Year's Day, I woke up, looked at my cane, and limped out of my room without it. I was done with it. The only time I would use it again would be at the end of exhausting days when my legs hurt too bad to walk without it. I also took it to therapy a couple of times, but that did not last long as Stephen would take it away. We traveled back home to Pensacola later on New Year's Day, to get ready to begin therapy again the next day. That time, my mom stayed in Georgia. Over the Christmas break, I drove by myself for the first time since the accident. It was nice to finally be able to drive again even if I was somewhat anxious. I was doing well enough to start taking care of myself, especially now that I could drive myself to therapy.

January had come, and there were a lot of things to get done. I had registered for my classes, but I still had not found a preceptor for the clinical hours, and time was running out. In fact, it wasn't until the day before I had to have everything set and ready to go that I finally found a preceptor. It was an answer to prayer, as I would have had to drop the class had I not found someone. Things were about to get hectic.

Work had resumed on the first of January. Class had started the week after that, and therapy was still three times a week for two hours. At the end of January, I would add on to this craziness 16 or more hours a week working in the clinic with my preceptor. As I looked at my schedule for the semester, it seemed impossible, especially with my lack of physical endurance and daily soreness.

I was discouraged as I began the first week of clinicals for grad school. During the weekend before, I had been in a lot of pain, and I just did not see how I could possibly be on my feet all day every day. I honestly did not know whether I would make it through the semester, but I could not focus on that. I had to take it a day at a time and trust that the Lord would give strength. When Monday came, surprisingly, the pain had lessened significantly and I felt much stronger than usual. I guess it should not have surprised me, because all through this trial, God had constantly proved His faithfulness to provide. He abundantly gave His grace not before I needed it or after I needed it but exactly when I needed it. Each week for the rest of the semester followed a similar pattern. Every Sunday, I would struggle as the week ahead seemed impossible, but by Monday, miraculously, I had the strength to face it.

My weeks were extremely busy. I woke up early every morning and usually did not make it to bed before midnight. My mornings and afternoons were filled with work, therapy, and clinicals, and my evenings were full of listening to lectures, studying, and working on projects. I had no time and honestly was too physically exhausted to cook meals, clean, and keep up with the house. Until that semester, Mom had been there to help keep up with all those things, but now it was just Michael and I. Again, I had such thoughtful friends and supporters in Pensacola who saw my need and came to my rescue.

Several of my coworkers cooked a lot of freezer meals for us, so we had easy, quick meals that would last most of the semester. Also, one of my nursing students organized groups of students to clean our house every weekend, and some volunteered to bring us a meal on the weekend. Many of my students signed up to help and often asked me whether they could do anything else to help us. Their support was overwhelming. I was very fortunate to have such great job with wonderful coworkers and students.

In the middle of that crazy semester, we had to head back to court in Troy, Alabama. This time, they would sentence the girl. By now, I was just ready for this to be completely finished. I did not look forward to going to court again, but I did look forward to meeting a few more of the men who helped to save our lives the night of the wreck. This court day would last much longer than the last one and be much more emotional, but at least when it was over, we would not have to go back again.

We spent time visiting our "new friends" at the fire station the evening before the sentencing. They told us of their remembrances from the wreck, and we enjoyed spending time with them and getting to know them. They were a bright spot in our visit to Troy.

April 4: First on our agenda was sitting down and conversing with the Assistant District Attorney, who would be representing the case. He discussed with us how he planned to proceed and told us that the judge we would have that day tended to be very lenient with her sentencing. Hearing that disturbed us some. He also asked who would be willing to testify. This time all of us would testify, including

Michael and both of my parents. I knew I would be reserved in what I said. I found it hard to relive the details and had long ago chosen not to focus on these things. I would be honest in what I said but most likely not overly detailed, which is why we decided it would be best to also allow my parents to testify.

As I entered the courtroom, I could already feel the emotional fatigue settling over me. The semester had exhausted me, and now I had to deal with conflicting emotions. As this day had approached, I had struggled often with how to handle this moment. On the one hand, I truly had resolved in my heart to forgive her and to hold no bitterness or anger against her, but did doing that mean I should not testify negatively against her? Should I beg the judge to show her mercy? On the other hand, I could not bear to think that someone else might have to go through what I had gone through or worse if she did not feel the gravity of the consequences for her choice to illegally drink and drive. This was not her first appearance in the courtroom in the past few years, which painted a picture for us that she did not take impactful decisions seriously. I settled in my heart to simply be honest and rely on what God laid on my heart to say when I took the stand. Ultimately, He was her judge.

The hearing lasted hours, with some very frustrating moments and very emotional moments. In an attempt to get us to feel sorry for her client, the defendant's attorney questioned me regarding the fact that I was working and back in school while her client could not even get a job or go back to school because of all that had taken place since the accident. I fought back emotions to angrily lash out. If only she knew what I had gone through to get where I was and how hard I had pushed to make it happen—how each night I fought to fall asleep as my legs throbbed from the stress I had put on them when they weren't strong enough to handle it. A lot of people in my situation would not have fought that hard; most would likely be on disability, spending their time at home. How could she turn the tables on me like that? I was not the one who irresponsibly chose to drink and drive. I did not choose to go through what I went through. The other driver had made that choice, and I was the one who suffered. Thankfully, God helped me to remain calm and gave me the words to say in response. I was relieved to finally step down from the stand.

My mom and dad followed me in their testimonies, leaving not a dry eye in the courtroom as they described what they had seen me go through and what they themselves emotionally had gone through. I hurt as I watched my dad fight back tears in describing the horrible nightmare they had gone through in almost losing me, the following painful battle as I struggled back to health, and the remaining hopes and dreams that might never come true. She had stripped away my youth, my first year of marriage, potentially my career, and likely my ability to ever become a mother. For the rest of my life, I would deal with pain and frustrations as a result of this accident that should have never happened. My parents and Michael truly helped to put in perspective how her decision had forever impacted my life. The courtroom was eerily silent as their testimonies finished, everyone feeling the emotional weight that had just been laid out in the open. The judge asked for a two-hour recess, after which she would give us her decision.

The two-hour wait seemed to stretch on forever. Finally, we gathered back in the courtroom. I was not prepared for what happened next. As the judge began, she looked at our family and said that she was sorry for what had happened and for the ruin to our lives, but she could not do anything to fix that or make it better. However, she could prevent another life from being ruined, and as a result, she would give some grace in her sentence. She looked at the girl who had hit us and told her what her sentence would be. She reminded her that she would be responsible for completing the sentence and that her parole officer would be keeping a close eye on her. She also told her to get a job, go back to school, and make the most of the lighter sentence she had been given.

I felt like I needed to pick my jaw up off the floor—not necessarily for the sentence the judge had given, because I had been prepared for that, but more so because of how she had basically said that she could not fix my life so she would help the person who had ruined my life have a good life. I thought maybe I was being a little too sensitive until after the case I heard others who had been in the courtroom fuming over her response to us. Of course, my parents also were upset with the response, but the sentence had been made. It was done and it was time to move on.

The car ride home was silent as we all processed what had happened and fought not to be bitter with the response we had received. Over the next few days, I struggled with anger about how things had been handled. For the rest of my life, I would remember vividly the day of the accident because of the pain and mobility issues I would deal with daily, and after completing her short sentence, the one who caused the accident would never have to think about it again! How was that fair? How did the judge think that fixing her life would solve anything? It was the girl's fault that I would have to live with and struggle through the effects of the accident. It was her choice to drink and then to drive. She should be the one suffering these consequences, not me! Finally, God brought to my remembrance that harboring anger and bitterness would only hurt me and that He had ultimately allowed the accident and allowed it for a reason. Temporarily, I had stopped focusing on the eternal and began focusing on the temporal. The girl might not have received what many people thought she deserved, but it was not our place to make that judgment. It was God's place to judge her, and His plan is always best.

My Journal Entries:

4/14/13: I am where I am today not because I am strong but rather because I have a God who is.

I must believe that my God is purposefully sovereign, because if He is not sovereign and perfecting His perfect will in my life, how can I see Him as always good in this difficult life? And if I do not see Him as good, how can I say He is love when life's difficulties so often flood in while I am just needing to rest in His arms? You see, if God is not sovereign, then He cannot be good. If God is not good, He cannot be love, and if God is not love, He would not be my Savior. Thank God for His sovereignty.

"But God..." —In my mind those are the most powerful words in Scripture (Genesis 50:20). It takes a hopeless, awful situation and adds an amazing all-powerful God, resulting in an immeasurably blessed future (Ephesians 2:2-7; Romans 5:8).

As the semester continued, my left knee continued to cause problems. The pain seemed to not be getting any better, and my knee kept locking on me. When I saw my leg surgeon in Birmingham, he recommended that I see a sports medicine doctor in Pensacola. He thought that I had a torn meniscus and that the best option would be for me to have surgery close to home. My therapist helped me get in pretty quickly with a good doctor, and not long after that, my surgery was scheduled for the first of May. In scheduling the surgery, there were quite a few things to work around: my job, taking my final for my graduate class and finishing my clinical hours, and having enough time to recover before having to start clinicals again at the end of May, as well as going to Birmingham to pass my physical assessment at the beginning of June. There was not a lot of time to get things worked out, but my doctor said it could it be done, so on May 1, I went back to surgery. The doctor removed the meniscal tear, cleaned out my knee, and removed some screws from both knees. The surgery went well, and the recovery was great! After the major surgeries I had already had, this one was a breeze, with minimal pain. I kept at my therapist, trying to get rid of the crutches that I had to use for a couple of weeks. Finally, I got permission to get rid of them and continued to make progress. The surgery did not help my pain much but did give me more range of motion with my knee, and I started having improvement in sitting down and getting up from chairs, which was definitely well worth the surgery and therapy. While therapy would continue for much of the summer, the summer would be focused on getting through the next graduate class.

My Journal Entries:

6/8/13: Faith. A small but intimidating word. What is true faith? Is it believing in something we see and can confirm, or is it something more? Hebrews 11:1 says, "Faith is the substance of things hoped for, the evidence of things not seen." It is easy to believe something when we are experiencing it in a tactile, obvious way, but real faith is seen when the subject of our faith seems an impossible reality yet our faith still remains unwavering. When I claim to be a Christian, I, in essence, state that I have faith in Christ and God the Father and the Holy Spirit and all that the Trinity claims to be. This faith springs from the Living Word, which God left on earth to share His gospel story, so my faith includes a belief in the inherent truth of the Word of God. If one concept in His Word is not true, then all my faith is vain because God has said that all Scripture was breathed from the mouth of God. In God's Word, He describes His complex and perfect character. It is faith in His perfect character that challenges me, often on a daily basis. It is easy for me to talk of my faith in God's love or sovereignty when I am experiencing happiness, wealth, and wisdom, but the real challenge comes when this is not the case. Faith is when I can be going through the darkest hour of life, when my body is wracked with shaking because of the immense pain it is in, and when I cannot close my eyes and sleep because I am afraid of what I will face when I wake up and can still say my God is love and my God is sovereign and all-powerful. If I cannot believe when I cannot see it, then my faith is still weak. If God is not love in the darkest hour, then my faith is not real. If every aspect of God's character is not true all the time, then God's Word is not true, and if God's Word is not true, then I have no foundation to my faith. If I have no foundation to my faith I am of all men most miserable, with a hopeless unbearable future.

At the beginning of June, we had to go to Birmingham for an on-site visit for my graduate class. During this time, I would have to pass a physical assessment and a Subjective, Objective, Assessment, and Plan (S.O.A.P.) note to be able to continue with the program. I hated pressured situations like that, as I never function as well as normal under those circumstances, but it would have to be done. As the day approached, I was nervous. I was under a time constraint that was generous, but I had to write my notes within that time frame.

With my left hand, my dominant hand, still weak from the nerve damage, I worried about being able to write quickly and legibly. A lot of prayer went into that day, and thankfully everything went relatively well. I was definitely glad to have that behind me. The rest of the summer, I focused on continuing to get stronger and learning all I could from the pediatric clinicals I was doing. It went by quickly, and before I knew it, fall semester was approaching.

The dreaded fall semester—all through my grad school, I had been dreading that semester. I would have to work part-time while completing 360 hours of clinicals and, for the first five weeks, take an intensive class. At the end of those five weeks, I would have to pass an exam to be able to graduate. As I looked at the semester ahead, it really seemed impossible, not just physically but time-wise. My schedule would be tight. I had 12 weeks to get in those 360 hours, and I did not know if it would happen. If I missed any day of clinicals, I would not finish my hours and would not be able to graduate. There literally was no room for getting sick or having anything happen that would prevent me from going to clinicals. As the semester approached, I began to feel overwhelmed, anxious, and discouraged. Physically, I still tired quickly and had quite a bit of pain. I wondered whether the semester would even be possible. Was I just plain crazy to be doing it?

A week before the craziness started, I hit a wall emotionally. I felt indescribably discouraged and overwhelmed at the impossible task ahead of me. I knew there was no way I could make it through the semester. I lay wide awake one night staring at the ceiling as once again the cares of this life had caused sleep to evade me. Tears began streaming down my face, and I began to tell God all about what was going on in my head. The feelings of discouragement, the embarrassment of always being stared at because of my scars, the feeling of being incapable to face the next semester, the absolute fatigue I had in fighting this never-ending battle, and the frustration of not being the wife for Michael that I wanted to be all came exploding out. Those things that had been bothering me for some time were finally coming to a head as I poured out my heart before God.

Over the summer, the frequent stares and whispers from people who saw my scars had gradually eaten away at my heart, causing me to want to avoid ever going out of the house. The constant focus on getting better and seemingly getting nowhere fast gradually wore down my determination, and the rigorous and demanding schooling while trying to work zapped what little strength I had left. I had been fighting that battle for so long and I was just exhausted. I was emotionally broken. I was reaching that home stretch, and I felt as if I had nothing left. I was tired—tired of fighting, tired of pushing, tired of life.

I knew I needed God's strength for that last, impossible semester. Not only that, but I needed to be reminded that He was there and that He loved me and that He had a plan. I begged Him for His strength to face the next months, and then I asked Him for one more thing. I asked Him to just send me a "token," something to remind me that He had a bigger purpose and a bigger plan. I needed to know He was still there, but I never could have imagined the big way He would answer that desperate prayer.

About a week later, as I walked out of therapy, the secretary asked whether she could talk to me for a moment. She told me that a reporter from the *The New York Times* had called and wondered whether he could have an interview with me. I could not believe what she just said! *The New York Times*?!? What did they want from me? I returned the reporter's call, and he told me that Terrell Thomas of the New York Giants had been inspired by my story. He said that it had helped him get back on the field. During my time at therapy, I had had the opportunity to meet several NFL players and various other athletes, all of whom were extremely nice. But Terrell had taken the time to mention me as part of his inspiration for getting back to what he loved, and the reporter wanted to include my story in his article. I talked with the reporter for quite some time, telling my story and sharing some about Terrell. At the end of the conversation, he asked me to e-mail him some pictures and said that when the article was published, he would send me the link. About midnight that night, I received the link to the article, and I could not help but smile. God had sent Terrell and that reporter as a direct answer to my prayer. Through it, He reminded me that He had a purpose for all I had gone through, that I might never know whose life I was affecting, that He loved me more than I could ever imagine, and that regardless of my choice to allow the cares of this world to discourage me, He would be there to pick me up and set me back on my feet.

The next morning, I woke up once again to my Facebook page blowing up with words of encouragement from those who had read the article. It was exactly the encouragement I needed to start the new semester on a good note. Since God had specifically and greatly answered my prayer for such a simple thing, I wondered how much more He would do through me during the coming semester.

As I had predicted, the semester was a blur! I had amazing preceptors who taught me a tremendous amount. One was a nurse practitioner who worked in nursing homes and psychiatric facilities and did home visits. This allowed me some great experience, and I learned a lot about being a good nurse practitioner and about life in general. The days I spent with her were long, but they allowed me to get in a lot of extra hours per day, which took some of the stress from the time crunch. I also worked with the hand surgeon who had fixed my elbow. I learned a tremendous amount from him and got some great experience. With such helpful clinicals, the semester actually ended up being enjoyable. It had helped that my coworkers, especially my friends Cheree and Jen, did all they could to help lighten the load and worked with my schedule. Before I knew it, my exit exam had come and gone and December had finally arrived. I finished my last day of clinicals on the first of December with barely enough hours. Now all I had left to do was finish the paperwork, send it in, and wait to see what my final grade would be. Also, during the semester, I had scheduled my nurse practitioner certification exam for two days before I was to walk for graduation. This was probably a little bit of a risky move, especially if I did not pass the certification exam, but I really wanted everything over and done with when I graduated.

Finally, I got my grade for the class. I had received an "A"! How amazing my God is! I had completed my M.S.N. with a 4.0! Now, I just needed to pass my certification exam and we could celebrate! I took my test on December 13. I had to travel to Tallahassee, Florida, to take the test, so I had stayed with my parents the night before. My dad drove me to the testing center that morning. As I sat in the van waiting to go in to take the test, my hands shook with nerves. A lot rested on the exam, and I had worked so hard for it. I would know at the end of the exam whether I had passed or not. My dad took my hands and prayed with me before I left the van. As I walked into the exam room, I continued to pray for peace and clarity as I thought through each question. Once I sat down, I took a deep breath, looked at the computer screen, and began the test. A little over an hour later, I completed the last question. I once again took a deep breath as I pushed the button to finish the exam, but the next screen was a survey that seemed to take forever! When I finished the survey, I was ready to see my results, but there was still one more screen that popped up. Finally, there was a button that said, "Push to see results." I quickly pushed the button and waited—and waited—and waited, as the screen kept "thinking." At last, the results popped up. I had passed! Relief washed over me as I realized my graduation would be a truly wonderful day of celebration!

December 14: The impossible day had come. Once again, we were back in Birmingham, but this time not for a doctor's appointment or for a stressful day of classes but for a day of celebration. Words cannot describe the emotions I had on that day. For the past nearly two years, I had put everything I had into that day becoming a reality. Many prayers from me and from hundreds of other people had gone into the day—prayers that had sustained me, encouraged me, and given me strength. That day, at the end of that phase of my life, I was a much different person than when I had begun. I was different spiritually, physically, and emotionally. Not just my family and I celebrated, but people from all around the world celebrated because a living, breathing miracle resulting from thousands of prayers prayed over the past two years WALKED across a stage in recognition of a completed degree that by human standards should have been impossible. And in that miraculous, special moment, it was proved that with God, my God, all things are possible.

I know no better way to end this story than to conclude with what God laid on my heart that morning of my graduation:

"I can do all things through Christ which strengtheneth me." Today, this verse takes on a new reality in my life. Just three days short of being two years after my accident, I will not ride in a wheelchair or use a walker or use a cane or even limp very noticeably across the stage but will WALK across the stage with a barely noticeable limp and receive a diploma that humanly speaking seemed an impossibility with my circumstances. But I serve and know the God of the impossible, and through His strength today, I achieve the impossible. It is God who deserves the glory, honor, and praise for this. As I look back over this year and see how God enabled and guided me, I am in awe. Thank you, Lord, for your supernatural strength and your guidance. May I never forget to give you praise for such great things you have done! Thank you also for an amazing family and friends who have supported, loved, and prayed for me and prayed that this day would be possible! May today, when I walk across the stage, be a testimony not of my abilities but of you and of your ability to achieve the impossible!"

May today and every day of my life be lived in awe and respect for the one who loved me, gave His life for me, and faithfully carried me through this valley.

Graduation day!

Taking a picture in front of the part of the hospital
where I did my therapy while in Birmingham

PART TWO
BROKENNESS BRINGS BEAUTY

CHAPTER 8

Timely Grace

*M*any times in my life, I can remember looking at people and wondering how they could ever deal with the difficulties and challenges that were placed in their lives. I remember questioning how they could live and cope daily with their hardships, because I did not think I ever could! In truth, I was right. In my own abilities, my own strength, or my own meager wisdom, I lack what is necessary to successfully face the ups and downs in this life. However, with a growing relationship with the Lord, I have all that I need to face all of life's challenges and to handle them in a God-honoring manner.

I have learned and am learning this truth as I continue to travel through this journey. Most of us are very familiar with II Corinthians 12:9, which reminds us that God's grace is sufficient for us. I believe that only through His grace alone can we begin to face the difficulties that are thrown our way. God's grace is bestowed on us daily, enabling us to walk the Christian walk, but it can be very difficult to really understand this grace and the power of its effectiveness until we are brought to a point of an absolutely desperate need for it—a point at which, without His grace, we cannot even fathom facing another hour. It is at this breaking point, this point of facing hopelessness, that we begin to experience the supernatural power of God's grace engulfing our lives and giving us the necessary resources to face our trials.

II Corinthians 12:9,10 states: "My grace is sufficient for thee: for my strength is made perfect in weakness. Most gladly therefore will I rather glory in my infirmities, that the power of Christ may rest upon me. Therefore I take pleasure in infirmities, in reproaches, in necessities, in persecutions, in distresses for Christ's sake: for when I am weak, then am I strong." This is such a beautiful passage. Because of my weakness, Christ's strength is perfected in me. Paul goes on to say that he takes pleasure in times of weakness because he realizes his inability allows God's ability and power to be evidenced. God's strength far exceeds our own, so it is in our times of weakness that we, through God's strength, truly are strong, and because of this, His grace is sufficient for all that we face.

I remember times throughout this trial that I felt engulfed by this grace, this strength! It truly is unexplainable. Often, I have found myself longing to experience again that feeling of intimacy with God that I had during the especially low moments at the beginning of this trial. In those moments, I knew that it was only His grace and strength that kept me breathing. I felt beloved, special, and worth saving to the One who created me and this entire universe. I would not trade those moments for the world.

Grace comes not a second before we need it or a second after we need it but exactly at the time that God knows we need it. It can be experienced in its full potential only when we choose to accept it. Just as when God in His grace offers His salvation, we are not blessed with this until we choose to accept it; the same applies to the grace bestowed in our everyday lives. We cannot take advantage of it until we allow God to use it in our lives. This requires a willingness to submit to God's will for our lives. We cannot truly experience His supernatural grace if we are not in alliance with Him. It is through this enabling grace that we can be successful in accomplishing His will for our lives.

My experience with God's supernatural grace is truly indescribable. It flooded the hospital rooms and encircled the many lives that were affected by my near-fatal accident. One of the main characteristics that stands out in my mind about that first hospital stay is peace and restfulness. When I first woke up, I was not overwhelmed at my circumstances but had a peace in my heart because I knew that God was palpably present and most certainly in control. All that happened was just a result of His grace. My circumstances were definitely worthy of causing an overwhelmed mind, yet through no ability of my own but through the grace of God on my life as a result of the prayers of God's people, I was able to peaceably rest through the two most trying weeks of my life.

God through His grace gave peace, so much so that even unsaved doctors and nurses noticed the difference in my family. Many comments were made about the peace that people sensed upon walking in my room. Throughout this trial, many people have remarked on the spirit in which this trial was handled. Well, I can say without a doubt in my heart that it was nothing of my or our doing. We could have never had the response we had if we were not saturated in God's grace. He enabled us to respond in a way that was pleasing and glorifying to Him. We simply had to choose to allow Him to work.

This is not saying that my response was always right. There were many times, more than I would like to admit, that I began to take my eyes off God and started focusing on my circumstances. It was during those times that I chose not to accept His grace but rather to enjoy wallowing in my own self-pity. However, even in those times of faltering, God's grace could be seen in His persistence to not give up on me. On those days when I was so steeped in a self-pity that seemed impossible to get out of, God would send a "token" to remind me He was still there if I would just let Him in. I did not deserve these reminders, but He still faithfully drew me back to Himself.

I would be wrong to not also point out God's grace in preparing me to face this trial. Five years prior to this tragedy, God knew what I would face in the future. He also knew that I had a lot of growing in my faith to do to be able to face this time.

God, in his sovereignty, allowed me to go through a difficult time in my life five years prior to the accident. That difficulty brought me to the point that I questioned even the validity of my faith. God had taken from me my fiancé at the time, along with the hopes and dreams that I had for my future. I felt hopeless and betrayed and frankly had no desire to live. My parents urged me to see a pastor friend of theirs. I knew I had nowhere else to turn, and I needed help. As I talked with that pastor, he pointed me to several passages of scripture. Through those passages, God opened my eyes to the realization that I had basically two choices: I could turn to the Sovereign God I had always trusted, who loved me and wanted only what was best for me, or I could choose to turn my back on this God who, regardless of what I thought, was still going to be sovereign and who ultimately controlled my life. Thankfully, God directed me to the right decision and through it caused me to realize how much my faith was lacking.

Growing up in a pastor's home, I came to know the Lord at an early age. I had learned how to talk and how to walk like a Christian, but instead of making my faith personal, I just relied on what everyone else told me I should believe and grew complacent in my relationship with the Lord. Eventually I realized that I needed to change—it was time I made my faith personal. I spent the next two summers at The Wilds Christian Camp, where God used the preaching of His Word, irreplaceable friends, and wise mentors to push me out of my complacency and challenge me daily to grow in my relationship with the Lord. He also led me to spend a year at a Bible college where I was able to immerse myself in Scripture and dedicate time to finding out what I believed and why I believed what I believed. During that time, God began developing in me a strong foundation in His sovereignty. I left that Bible college with a firm assurance that God was in control of my life and that He was worth trusting, regardless of my circumstances. Little did I know that just a few years later, that faith would be an absolute necessity as I would be tried by fire.

What an amazing God I have, who years before foresaw what I would need and prepared me for it. II Peter 1:3 comes to my mind every time I think of this divine preparation. It states, "According as his divine power hath given unto us all things that pertain unto life and godliness, through the knowledge of him that hath called us to glory and virtue." I had studied the book of II Peter for one of the projects I had to complete for Bible college, and this verse really made an impact on me. This verse promises that God will give believers all we need to live our lives and, not only that, but live lives that are godly. In my mind, the next verse I think of is I Corinthians 10:13. "There hath no temptation taken you but such as is common to man; but God is faithful, who will not suffer you to be tempted above that ye are able; but will with the temptation also make a way to escape, that ye may be able to bear it." God, in His sovereignty, prepared me years ago to face my trial and gave me the tools necessary to successfully face the hardship and resist or escape the many temptations that came with it. I just had to choose to let Him be in control. This is easy to say, but much harder to do, and unfortunately, many times I made the wrong choice. However, God remained faithful, and regardless of my wrong choices, He did a great work in my life.

While years before the accident God's grace was at work, it also was at work from the second the wreck happened. Yes, God allowed my car to be hit, but we immediately saw His hand. In the car directly behind us was an off-duty EMT and his wife. They were our first responders, not just physically but also spiritually. As the EMT assessed the scene and got emergency personnel there as quick as possible, his wife began praying that God would spare our lives. That was the first of thousands of prayers that would go up for my life over the next few weeks, months, and years—prayers that, as you have hopefully seen, would make all the difference. God's grace was, is, and always will be sufficient.

CHAPTER 9

Forgiven

*F*orgiven—that is what I am. I am forgiven of all my sins. I am totally undeserving of this forgiveness. Nothing I have done warrants this, but I still have been the recipient of unconditional, complete forgiveness. And not only that, I can have this forgiveness because God sacrificed his only Son to be beaten, ridiculed, and killed by the very people for whom He sent His Son to provide forgiveness and salvation. What an amazing sacrifice, and yet we as humans have trouble forgiving petty, little offenses committed against us!

Often I have been asked about my feelings toward the girl who hit me. Of course, with all that happened, forgiveness is something that is difficult. Through this time, I have really begun to see that forgiveness is not just a one-time choice; we must daily, or maybe even hourly, make the choice to forgive. It is a choice to not dwell on the negative actions that have been committed towards me. When I have a rough, painful, discouraging day, forgiveness is the choice to not be angry and to not continue to place hateful blame on the drunk driver. It is an active, constant choice, but a choice that must be made and made correctly. So how do we make this correct choice? The answer is simple, but putting it into practice can be difficult.

Forgiveness requires focus. We have to keep our focus glued on Christ and on eternity. We must focus on the forgiveness we have received and continue to receive, remembering that we do not deserve it. Because of our sins—because of MY sins—the life of Christ was required and was freely given, and through that sacrifice, we have forgiveness of our numerous sins. Focusing on this truth helps me to see how undeserving I am to receive forgiveness. It also serves as a reminder that if my purpose in life is to be like Christ, how can I possibly choose not to forgive, even if that person is undeserving of forgiveness?

A focus on God's sovereignty is also necessary. If I remember that God had a plan for all that happened and allowed it to happen, then I should not have unforgiveness. Choosing to not forgive is choosing to be angry and bitter with God and His choice for my life.

In contemplating forgiveness, several questions came to my mind, particularly in regards to testifying at the trial and how Christ and forgiveness should be portrayed. I struggled with getting up on the stand and stating that I believed she should be punished for her choice. As I thought on this, the Lord brought a thought to my mind. We are always very quick to focus on God's goodness, mercy, love, and forgiveness, which are wonderful characteristics to dwell on. But many times when we focus on these, it blurs the reality that God is also just and that there are consequences for our choices. We may be a forgiven child of God and going to spend eternity in Heaven with Him, but that does not mean that while on earth, we will not suffer consequences for the wrong choices we make. It also does not mean that we will be spared from the consequences of a fallen world in which we live. In showing forgiveness to the girl who hit me, I am choosing to not hold against her what she has done to me personally. I am choosing to pray for her rather than to hate her. I am choosing not to dwell on how she has negatively impacted my life but rather to love and care for her spiritual state. However, my forgiveness of her actions does not mean that she should not suffer the consequences of her mistake. The consequences of our actions are a way in which we learn to not repeat those actions. God often uses consequences to form us into people better fit for serving Him. We must face the reality that our choices have consequences. I could still show God's love while on that witness stand with the words I chose and the attitude I had, realizing that were she not to suffer consequences for her choices, her actions might not change and the next person she hit might not be as fortunate as I was.

However, ultimately, I must choose to forgive her—daily, if needed. I have been forgiven of so much, and I have no right not to forgive her. Forgiveness and love are gifts that I have freely been given, and gifts I have been charged to share with others. Regarding bitterness and anger towards her only makes me miserable and harms my relationship with Christ. Nothing is worth sacrificing that essential relationship. Through God's grace, I can choose forgiveness.

CHAPTER 10

The Hardest Battle

*W*henever someone goes through a traumatic experience resulting in extensive physical injuries, their first response is to focus on the physical difficulties, often forgetting the emotional aspect of the traumatic event. I will not deny that the physical pain and agony were excruciating at times, but I think, overall, that the emotional and mental battle was a much more difficult fight for me. It was and is still a daily, oftentimes hourly, unrelenting assault on my mental-well being—a fight that I would without question succumb to without a relationship with Christ.

During the first few months after the accident, when my physical state was so variable, dealing with my emotions was pushed to the back of my mind as I fought just to stay alive. The support of family, friends, churches, and thousands of people whom I did not even know was indescribable. I felt enveloped in undeserved love and care, and that support carried me through those first few months. I cannot imagine going through my traumatic experience without that tremendous support; however, the "newness" of my trauma eventually began to wear off, and a full-on assault on my mind and attitude began.

From nearly the beginning of my consciousness after the accident, I knew that the emotional battle would be the hardest battle I would have to fight. From the years I spent working at The Wilds Christian Camp and the time I spent working on a master's of biblical counseling at Northland International University, I knew what was essential for being victorious in this battle, but knowing and implementing are two different things. So many verses raced into my head to reinforce the thinking I should have: Proverbs 3:5-6, Matthew 6:33-34, Philippians 4, James 1, and I Peter 1:7. However, the real test was whether or not I could place my faith in Christ to give me the strength to implement these principles.

As mentioned in the story previously, I really felt the power of this battle right around the first Valentine's Day, followed by the discouragement at my birthday. Then the bad news about my ex-fix came, followed by my inability to walk after the ex-fix came off. That was followed by questions about being able to start grad school and then seemingly the lack of strength to complete the last stretch of grad school. All of these times, I battled a deep, dark discouragement, and each time I had to come to a point where I chose to hand it over to God and let Him handle it.

The emotional battle is such a tough battle because it is in our minds. Often it starts out unnoticed and gradually grows to the point where it seems impossible to get rid of. That is the danger of this discouragement, this "mental" battle. The battle is in the mind, and so often the beginning of this battle is fought without being evidenced to those around us. By the time we begin to evidence the effects of losing this battle, we have spiritually already given up much ground.

This mental battle takes away the safeguard of confrontation. No one knows the thoughts we are struggling with and therefore cannot confront the wrong thinking. For people like me who struggle to talk about what is going on in their head, this struggle becomes a dangerous battlefield spiritually — one that must be protected against and one that the Bible does address in Philippians 4. Paul reminds us to be "careful for nothing" and to bring our requests to God "through prayer and supplication with thanksgiving." He goes on in Philippians 4:8 to tell us what we should be focusing on. I had to learn to choose to dwell only on things that are "true, honest, just, pure, lovely, and of good report" or I would and still often do begin to lose the battle. The discouraging thoughts and lies of Satan regarding my circumstances will come, but it is my choice to choose not to dwell on them.

I am amazed as I look back over this journey and see how many times I have slipped in this battle, but even in those times of weakness, God still remained faithful. In fact, it was often in those times when He revealed in a great way His personable, intimate, and specific love for me. I have referred to many of these reminders of His constant love, care, and concern for me as my "tokens" from Him. I shared one of these "tokens" in the story, when I got the call from *The New York Times* reporter, but there were many more, and I would like to share one more.

The first "token" came shortly after being discharged from the hospital when I had had a really tough day. It came in the form of an e-mail to my dad. Attached with the e-mail was this poem. I have read it many times since then as a reminder of God's bigger plan.

The Master Weaver's Plan

My life is but a weaving
Between the Lord and me;
I may not choose the colors–
He knows what they should be.

For He can view the pattern
Upon the upper side
While I can see it only
On this, the under side.

Sometimes He weaves in sorrow,
Which seems so strange to me;
But I will trust His judgment
And work on faithfully.

'Tis He who fills the shuttle,
And He knows what is best;
So I shall weave in earnest,
And leave to Him the rest.

Not 'til the loom is silent
And the shuttles cease to fly
Shall God unroll the canvas
And explain the reason why.

The dark threads are as needed
In the Weaver's skillful hand

As the threads of gold and silver
In the pattern He has planned.

—Author Unknown (*Meet Me in the Meadow*)

I cannot wait for that day when the Lord unrolls the canvas so I can see how He has used these dark threads in my life to create a beautiful picture. This poem has often been an encouragement and a reminder of the brevity of this life compared to eternity, and the importance of keeping my focus on making a difference for eternity.

In addition to this poem, there was a song that I listened to many times. The song, *Blessings*, by Laura Story, brought great encouragement to me, helping me to keep my focus and to look for the good in this trial. Blessings do not always come in the form of "good" as defined by this world. Often the blessing comes from the struggle, from the times when, because of our utter dependence on God, we feel and know His strength in a very real way, and as a result, our faith grows; times when, because of our struggles, we feel the love and support of so many people, even those whom we do not know; times when, because of our struggles, we long for eternity, to be home with our Savior; and times when, because of our struggles, we see impossible things become possible because of our great God. Through our trials, God's greatness is revealed. I love this song because it describes perfectly what this trial often has meant to me. I have had those sleepless nights crying out in anger when it seemed He had disappeared, those times when I wondered whether He still loved me and where His goodness was, and those times when I thought I would never crawl out of such dark discouragement. But truly, as the song says, those times were blessings in disguise, used to draw me close to my Savior, to cultivate in me a longing to be home with Him, and to reveal in a real way how truly awesome my God is.

While I have come a long way in this emotional battle, there will still be battles to face. Recently, the hardest struggles have come with the embarrassment of being stared at because of how I am different. The scars, particularly on my leg, are rather disfiguring, and my gait still has a limp. Each time I am out in public, especially during the hot, humid summer here in Florida, people stare. I watch as people, sometimes discreetly and sometimes not so discreetly, stare at my scars, often making disgusted faces probably without realizing it. Occasionally, someone will ask me what happened. I always appreciate when that happens. At least it gives me an opportunity to share a brief version of my story. The stares do often trigger in my mind thoughts of discouragement as I struggle with insecurity and no longer feeling beautiful—again an area in which I must keep my focus on Christ and His view of me rather than how the world views me.

There are many other difficult emotional battles that I face and in the future will face again. Each battle brings its own unique challenges, but with each battle, there will be just one right focus— keeping my focus on Christ and His better plan for my life can bring victory to even my hardest battle.

CHAPTER 11

Broken But Beautiful

$\mathcal{P}$erhaps you have been wondering where the title I gave this book came from. I gave it quite a lot of thought and eventually came to land on this title. In my mind, it describes in totality the struggles and resolutions of this valley. It encompasses the physical, emotional, and spiritual aspects of this time.

Physically, the Lord allowed me to be broken. In fact, He allowed this earthen vessel to be literally shattered into a million pieces, but only because He had a plan. Emotionally, the Lord allowed brokenness. He allowed the pain of no longer being viewed as normal, the frustration of losing that first special year of marriage, the disappointment of losing my youth and no longer being able to run a marathon, play beach volleyball with my friends, or climb mountains with my sister in Hawaii. He allowed the embarrassment of never being able to go out in public again without facing disgusted stares at the scars that cover my left side and the discouragement of never truly feeling beautiful again. And, lastly, spiritually, the Lord allowed brokenness. He brought me to the point of absolute desperation. I had to trust Him. Only He could perform miracles and give me the strength I needed to reach my dreams. I was forced to grow in my faith because He was my only hope. **Brokenness** defined me in this trial.

However that was not where the story ended, because God had a bigger plan than a broken, shattered vessel. He began to piece by piece put me back together again into a beautiful vessel better used for His service. Physically, He strengthened when strength was needed, provided the right medical help when help was needed, and gave healing when the timing was perfect. Each day that I place my foot on the ground and take a step, I am a walking example of God's beautiful grace. Emotionally, He encompassed me with love, peace, and perseverance. He showered blessings, provided for every need, and reminded me of His love with His "tokens for good" when I needed them most. Spiritually, He grew my faith by showing me and all those who were watching His beautiful, miraculous grace. He was never failing and always faithfully there. **Beautiful** defined God and His grace in this trial.

You may be wondering why I use the term "beautiful," and simply put, this is why: Beautiful, because His grace painted a picture of His love for me. Beautiful, because He touched not only my life, but thousands of lives around the world. Beautiful, because all along, He had a bigger plan that we got to watch unfold. And beautiful, because although in the eyes of those who do not know my story, my scars are ugly, to those who do know my story, they are a beautiful reminder of God's grace in my life. In God's eyes, I am still beautiful. I am His beautiful creation. My beautiful scars are evidence of His **S**ufficient grace that **C**arried me and His **A**mazing grace that **R**evealed in me **S**upernatural strength for each day.

Works Cited

Boyd, Travis L. "God is Faithful." Lyrics. Perf. Sons of Jubal. *God is Faithful*. The Lorenz Corporation, 2003. CD.

"The Master Weaver's Plan." *Meet Me in the Meadow*. 1, February 2012. www.meetmeinthemedow.com.

CPSIA information can be obtained
at www.ICGtesting.com
Printed in the USA
FSOW02n1319051116
27015FS